FAMILY AND DELINQUENCY
Resocializing the Young Offender

FAMILY AND DELINQUENCY
Resocializing the Young Offender

Ludwig L. Geismar, Ph.D.

Katherine M. Wood, Ph.D.

Rutgers University
School of Social Work
New Brunswick, New Jersey

HUMAN SCIENCES PRESS, INC.
72 FIFTH AVENUE
NEW YORK, N.Y. 10011

Copyright © 1986 by Human Sciences Press, Inc.
72 Fifth Avenue, New York, New York 10011

Printed in the United States of America
987654321

Library of Congress Cataloging in Publication Data

Geismar, Ludwig L.
  Family and delinquency.

  References: p. 219
  Includes index.
  1. Rehabilitation of juvenile delinquents.
2. Juvenile delinquents—Family relationships.
I. Wood, Katherine. II. Title.
HV9085.G45 1986   364.3'6   85-8278
ISBN 0-89885-245-5

CONTENTS

ACKNOWLEDGMENTS

In gathering the material for this volume we have become indebted to a number of people. Angela Waff, Long Term Care Systems Analyst of the New Jersey Department of Human Services, helped us review the literature bearing on the relationship between family and juvenile delinquency. Former graduate students Lori Provost, Lisa DeHope, Laura Eure, Elissa Schwartz, and Richard Briefstein carried out extensive field interviews, often under much less than ideal conditions in terms of comfort and safety.

We wish to thank the Honorable Robert Wilentz, Chief Justice of the New Jersey Supreme Court, for facilitating access to correctional systems data; and Robert Lipscher, Administrative Director of the Courts, and Dr. Marshall Whithed, Legal Systems Analyst, for making the administrative arrangements for the data collection.

A special note of thanks goes to Lou Csabay, former Administrator, Passaic Intake Service, and Shirley M.

Kayne, Coordinator, Family Counseling Unit, for providing research facilities and lending material and moral support to the study.

Jill Schumann, doctoral candidate in history at Rutgers University, gave us a big helping hand with editorial suggestions, and Barbara Molnar was forever responsive to demands for unreasonable typing deadlines.

We also gratefully acknowledge the financial support of the Rutgers Research Council.

All names and other identifying information have been fictionalized throughout the text. Resemblance to any persons, living or dead, is not intended.

Chapter 1

INTRODUCTION

The family's role in the genesis and control of juvenile delinquency is recognized widely. A good deal of popular literature, journal articles, clinical writing, social welfare case studies, and police reports provide evidence of the connection between disturbed family situations and the deviant behavior of young people emerging from these family backgrounds. It is therefore surprising that relatively little effort has been devoted to systematic study and related writing about the interrelationships between the two phenomena.

The most plausible explanation for this state of affairs is the discipline separation of the family and crime study areas. Families have been studied by anthropologists, sociologists, an occasional social and clinical psychologist, and, in a highly focused way, by home economists, lawyers, and general economists. Juvenile delinquency has been the concern of criminal justice, law, and sociology. The sociologists who have devoted most effort to research and scholarship in both areas, family as well as delinquency, have pursued these interests within the framework of fairly separate subdisciplines: family sociology and the sociology of social deviance and control. This separation is reflected in the formulation of college curricula and in the structuring of professional activities at conferences and in the publishing field.

Divisions among academic disciplines and subdisciplines do not denote an abnormal situation. They are an essential part of the structure that allows for specialization with regard to research, knowledge building, and training in given fields of study. Inevitably, however, divisions also serve to inhibit the pursuit of knowledge, as James D. Watson (1968) intimated when he learned to jump discipline boundaries on his way to discovering the structure of the DNA.

Sheldon and Eleanor Glueck (1950) and F. Ivan Nye (1958 and 1973) furnish an example of how the frontiers between criminology and family sociology can be crossed successfully to produce substantial studies linking the fields theoretically. Family variables, mainly of a structural nature, have been utilized by many writers on the subject of juvenile deviant behavior. Family sociologists have recently taken stock of the relationship between family life and deviant behavior (Bahr, 1979).

The present volume is written from an applied perspective. Its goal is the cumulation of knowledge that may lead to more effective approaches for coping with juvenile delinquents. The apparent salience of family factors in the rehabilitation of juvenile offenders was brought home in a recent study involving one of the authors (Coull, Geismar, & Waff, 1982), in which family functioning and the family's relationship to the young probationer were very significantly related to recidivism. A review of the existing literature on the subject of family and delinquency revealed converging evidence of the role of family in the etiology as well as the control of juvenile deviant behavior. A number of delinquency treatment programs scattered throughout the country have taken family life as a point of reference in intervention, but there is very little systematic research on outcomes. Treatment programs tend to be established without undue concern for theoretical issues or empirical evidence. In defense of this approach one might argue that social problems do not wait for the maturing of scholarship. However correct that assessment may be, the actual cost of trying to solve problems by applying inappropriate or ineffective methods may well outweigh the presumed benefits of timely intervention.

The authors of the present volume take the unequivocal position that services and policies should be the end result of a process that examines theoretical relevance and draws on empirical evidence with a direct bearing in the field. The end result is likely to be not a definitive prescription for treatment but an intervention model, the efficacy of which can be tested in terms of the criteria of outcome that are allied with the model.

The caution expressed relative to any proposed strategy of intervention must be extended to include a warning about the cure-all potential of family treatment. The field of juvenile delinquency has been subjected to close scrutiny with the aid of numerous theoretical and empirical investigations that collectively have demonstrated the multivariate etiology of the problem. Few people will be tempted to seek in the family either the single cause of juvenile deviant behavior or the only arena in which treatment can be successfully undertaken. The point of the present statement is rather that the family variable has been grossly neglected in the social and behavioral science literature and that the professional treatment field has given it unsystematic attention at best. It is the writers' goal, then, to contribute to a reversal of these trends and to stimulate researchers and practitioners toward endeavors that tap the intricate connections between family and juvenile delinquency.

We shall seek to accomplish this objective by first reviewing the literature that juxtaposes juvenile delinquency and a variety of family variables. Our next concern is the relative significance of selected family factors in the etiology of delinquency. That discussion is linked to an attempt to identify family functioning patterns as they bear on efforts to resocialize juvenile offenders. This will be followed by a critical review of family treatment programs aimed at the control or prevention of deviant behavior among young people. Finally, the process of sorting out theoretical writings and empirical data collected by the authors leads to the beginning formulation of a model for intervention aimed at rehabilitating the young delinquent.

Chapter 2

FAMILY VARIABLES DEALING WITH JUVENILE DELINQUENCY

The literature is replete with efforts, spanning decades, to determine the relationship between juvenile delinquency and family variables. Sociological studies have focused primarily on structural variables such as family size, broken home, social class, and employment status of parents (for instance, Cohen, 1955; Glueck & Glueck, 1950; Lees & Newsom, 1954; Monahan, 1957; Shaw & McKay, 1932; Slocum & Stone, 1963). Psychological and psychiatric research has been largely limited to intra- and interpersonal dynamics drawn from clinical experience (for example, Aichhorn, 1935; Bowlby, Ainsworth, Boston, & Rosenbluth, 1956; Eissler, 1949; Friedlander, 1947; Johnson, 1949). Numerous competing single variable theories have emerged (anomie, labeling, differential association, and so on) whose advocates have a predominantly sociological identification (Merton, 1949; Schur, 1971; Sutherland, 1939).

Efforts at integrating into an empirically defensible framework the identified sociological and psychological correlates that link the family and juvenile delinquency are of recent origin (Bahr, 1979; Johnson, 1979). The failure to recognize different sources of delinquency and to articulate a comprehensive framework has undoubtedly restricted success in some studies (Rodman & Grams, 1967, pp. 203–205). Becker's (1963) assessment of 16 years ago, valid now as it was then, points to an additional problem:

> There simply are not enough studies that provide us with facts about the lives of delinquents. Many studies correlate the incidence of delinquency with such factors as kind of neighborhood, kind of family life, or kind of personality. Very few tell us in detail what a juvenile delinquent does in his daily round of activity and what he thinks about himself, society, and his activities. (p.166)

There is, indeed, a paucity of research that considers simultaneously the intrafamilial mechanisms and the intrapersonal dynamics of the delinquent, or that adequately explores the cause-and-effect relationships between family function variables and delinquent behavior (Bahr, 1979; Gable & Brown, 1978; Langner, McCarthy, Gersten, Simcha-Fagan, & Eisenberg, 1979).

STRUCTURAL VARIABLES

Among family variables that have received the broadest attention over the longest period of time, *structure* occupies first place. Its ready availability undoubtedly accounts for its extensive use. The main structural variables that have been investigated in connection with juvenile delinquency are family size, birth order, broken homes, and working mothers.
Of these four, family size has been given least attention because of its close correlation with other variables, such

as poverty and certain types of ecological and ethnic characteristics, and also because family size has been fluctuating over time. The Gluecks (1950, pp. 93–95, 119) and Slocum and Stone (1963) identified family size as a factor in delinquent behavior, and so did Nye (1973, pp. 38, 56–58), even where mother's employment status was controlled. Reiss (1952) found that a greater proportion of delinquents from large families had poor ego structures, and Hirschi (1971, pp. 239–241) reported that total number of children in the family is correlated with juvenile delinquency. Others who in recent years have found family size to be associated with delinquency include Andrew (1976) and Biles (1971).

Birth order also has been examined relative to delinquent behavior, and available evidence points to intermediary children being overrepresented in the delinquent population (Biles, 1971; Glueck & Glueck, 1950, p. 120; Lees & Newsom, 1954; Nye, 1973, p. 37). Nye's own data showed that both the youngest siblings and the intermediaries are more likely to become delinquents. Haskell and Yablonsky's explanation (1974, p. 103) with regard to the in-between children is that they get squeezed out of the family into gangs because the parents tend to give more attention to the oldest and youngest offspring. Hirschi, however, reaches the more general conclusion that there is only an erratic relationship between delinquency and ordinal positions when family size is controlled (1971, p. 241).

In a society that has traditionally considered the two-parent home as the norm and the optimum environment for raising children, broken homes have been viewed as a potential source of trouble by lay persons and social scientists alike. Robison (1960) reports that the U.S. Children's Bureau published statistics for as early as 1928 showing that 29 percent of all boys and 48 percent of all girls brought to court were not living with both parents (p. 109). She cites even earlier Census Bureau statistics indicating that in 1923 almost one out of two children (46 percent) in institutions came from broken homes. Studies done in California (Mathews, 1923) and Oklahoma (Sullenger, 1930) also demonstrated that about half of the delinquents in two studies originated in broken homes. Shulman (1949) and Smith (1955) also found broken homes related to juvenile delinquency but less crucially than family discord and deficient parent-child relationships (Shulman) or poverty, social disorganization, and differential treatment by law enforcement and social agencies (Smith). Slocum and Stone (1963), who surveyed students in several public high schools with the aid of a questionnaire, established a clear link between broken homes and "delinquency type behavior" (violation of certain conventions and laws).

One of the most widely cited among the early research studies on delinquency and broken homes is the work of Shaw and McKay (1931), who interviewed the families of 7,278 boys aged ten to seventeen in 29 Chicago schools and 1,675 boys who had appeared in Cook County Court. Rate of broken homes generally correlated with age of boy and also was associated with ethnicity, but it showed no significant relationship to juvenile delinquency. Extensive data analysis led the researchers to conclude that broken homes as such are not as important a factor in delinquency causation as the cumulative effect of family discord.

Monahan (1957), who compared 44,448 appearances of 36,245 boys and girls in the Philadelphia Municipal Court, found that there was a greater proportion of repeat appearances in every type of broken home than in unbroken homes. McCord, McCord and Zola (1959, p. 83) and Nye (1973, p. 47), using multivariate analyses, report no difference in delinquent behavior between those whose homes were broken before age five and those whose homes were broken later. On the other hand, Nye's (1973) research relying on student questionnaires did find that children of broken homes are overrepresented in state institutions and that they commit slightly more delinquent

behavior in high school than those from unbroken homes
(pp. 47–48). Neither investigator, however, was able to
identify the broken home per se as a causative factor in
juvenile delinquency. A similar conclusion was reached by
Kraus and Smith (1973) who had compared recidivist and
nonrecidivist juvenile delinquents in Australia.

Richard Sterne (1964), who also addressed this subject,
reviewed the files of 1,050 white juveniles appearing before
the Mercer County, New Jersey, Juvenile Court. His data
failed to show a significant relationship between broken
homes and delinquency as measured by serious offense (pp.
74–92). By contrast, Chilton and Markle (1972) on the basis
of an analysis of Florida juvenile court data in 1969 reported a clear-cut association between family disruption
and juvenile delinquency as well as seriousness of offense.

Hirschi (1971) in a more recent study in the San Francisco–Oakland metropolitan area (the study comprised
4,000 students studied by means of questionnaires and
school and police records) contrasted juvenile court statistics with self-reporting on delinquent acts. He found only
those living with step- or foster fathers to be more likely
than children from intact homes to be delinquent. However, self-reporting showed only a weak relationship between broken homes and delinquency, and Hirschi views
this finding to be consistent with other research on this
subject (pp. 242–243; see particularly Hennessy, Richards,
& Berk, 1978). The combined evidence reviewed here does
not make an impressive case for the broken home being a
causative factor in juvenile delinquency, particularly when
the delinquency variable is defined in ways other than official statistics and when influences such as poverty and
social disorganization are held constant.

Haskell and Yablonsky (1974), in reviewing eight significant studies extending over nearly half a century on
the effects of broken homes on juvenile delinquency, found
that the direction (though not the magnitude or statistical

significance) is the same in all these studies. Broken homes showed an association with juvenile delinquency. At the same time they were also led to conclude "that it is not the absence of a parent per se that is associated with delinquency but rather the kind of relationship that exists between children and remaining parents" (pp. 100–101).

Among more recent studies only Andrew (1976) seems to make a clear case for a broken home–delinquency nexus, whereas the findings of Hennessy, Richards, and Berk (1978) and Ensminger, Kellam, and Rubin (1983), in line with the results of most investigators cited above, see only small effects of family structure on juvenile delinquency.

The notion of working mothers as a cause of juvenile delinquency springs from the same social norm as the assumption that broken families cause delinquency: that of the two-parent family where the mother stays home as a full-time nurturer and socializer of children. By implication the mother working outside the home, particularly the gainfully employed woman, is seen as likely to fail in these functions, a failure that may result in delinquency of an offspring.

The Gluecks, who compared the relative frequency of working mothers among delinquents and nondelinquents (1957), claimed to have identified a "deleterious influence" on the family life and on the children of some working mothers. They also reported that the mothers of delinquents worked more sporadically than the mothers of nondelinquents, leading the researchers to the conclusion that these mothers were less effective with their children. Maccoby (1958), after reanalyzing these data and taking into account the variable supervision of the child, arrived at an interpretation that pinpointed the quality of child care as the key variable in juvenile delinquency.

Nye (1973), who had tested the relationship of juvenile delinquency to a large number of family variables, discovered a substantial relationship between mothers' employment and delinquency of offspring. Nevertheless, when Nye held constant the broken homes factor and a number of other social background variables, the differences between children of working and nonworking mothers, although still in the direction indicated above, lost statistical significance (pp. 53–59).

The Sterne research mentioned previously (1964) found serious offenses totally unrelated to the work status of the mother (p. 67). Hirschi (1971), more in line with Nye's findings, saw "the relationship between mother's employment and delinquency not particularly strong, but the linearity of the relation, from full-time employment to part-time to housewife, suggests that some aspect of direct supervision and not some characteristic of the mother or of the child accounts for the relation" (p. 236). Hirschi's multiple regression analysis of his data, when various antecedent variables were controlled, indicated that the relationship between mother's employment and delinquency persists (p. 238). Hirschi speculates that in addition to maternal supervision, geographical proximity of the working mother may help explain the relationship.

The search for structural variables as correlates of juvenile delinquency has yielded positive and reasonably consistent findings with low explanatory power. In other words, variables such as mother's employment or parent absence are clearly correlated with the delinquent behavior of children. Yet other factors associated with the structural one reduce or eliminate the original correlation and serve as plausible explanations of the delinquent behavior. Thus, the nature of parental love or supervision in the home can tell us more about the likelihood of a youngster becoming a delinquent than the presence of one or two parents. And conversely, a favorable home atmosphere can do much to neutralize the somewhat adverse affect of having only one parent in the home.

These findings clearly point the way to pursuing the

subject of family variables affecting delinquency, not in structural terms but from the perspective of psychosocial behavior and functioning that captures the underlying dynamic of family life.

FAMILY FUNCTIONING VARIABLES

It should be noted that studies spanning more than three decades have addressed this subject and the investigators associated with such research include Andry (1971), Dentler and Monroe (1961), the Gluecks (1950, 1962, 1968), Johnson (1979), Nye (1973), Slocum and Stone (1963).

The literature dealing with family functioning variables with a bearing on juvenile delinquency can best be categorized under the following headings: (1) parental affection/acceptance versus rejection, (2) family relationships, (3) parental supervision/discipline, and (4) family deviance including social disorganization. These are not truly mutually exclusive conceptualizations but categories under which the existing literature can be most readily classified.

Parental Affection/Acceptance

Delinquency research inquiring into the expressive relationships between parents and children was greatly influenced by Bowlby's well known study *Maternal Care and Mental Health* (1952). Bowlby saw the mother-child relationship as a key element in human development. The child needs the warm feeling that derives from this relationship, and he/she is likely to suffer maternal deprivation if warmth is absent. Length of deprivation and age at which it is experienced determine the extent of the damage, which may include hostility toward the mother, excessive demands, shallow emotional attachment, and apathy or withdrawal.

During the same period the Gluecks (1950, 1962) had been comparing delinquent and nondelinquent groups of boys on a wide range of parent-child relationships in a search for causative links to juvenile delinquency. Their data indicated the presence of more hostility and less affection between parents and boys in the delinquent group (1962, pp. 125–129).

Using a much smaller sample of delinquent and nondelinquent boys, Bandura and Walters (1959) found similar indications: the parents, particularly the fathers, of the delinquent boys were more rejecting and less affectionate than the parents of the nondelinquent subjects. The researchers noted that the fathers of the delinquent boys were quick to ridicule their sons and that between fathers and sons there existed an overall ambiance of hostility.

Nye (1973) in studying degrees of parent-child acceptance/rejection (mutual and unilateral) found that rejection of the child by the parent (and vice versa) is related strongly to juvenile delinquency. Of the 313 cases of mother-child mutual rejection, 48 percent of the children were in Nye's "most delinquent" category, and of 292 cases of mutual acceptance only 14 percent were in that category. Results of the father-child acceptance/rejection measures were very similar. Nye concluded that mutual acceptance or mutual rejection between parent and child is more closely related to delinquent behavior than an acceptance/ rejection combination (pp. 75–76).

Andry (1962, pp. 349–350, 1971, pp. 27–41), also investigated parental acceptance/affection as it related to small samples (about 80 each) of delinquent and nondelinquent youths. His findings (1962) pointed to a clear-cut differentiation between delinquents and nondelinquents in their perceptions of parental, affective roles:

The delinquent youths tended to feel more loved by
their mothers; the nondelinquent youths tended to
feel loved by both parents.

The delinquent group tended to feel that their parents, fathers especially, were embarrassed to show
affection for them openly, and the youths themselves felt embarrassment at showing open affection
for their parents.

The delinquent youths tended to feel parental hostility
toward them.

Similar findings regarding the nexus between juvenile delinquency and familial affection and closeness came from
the studies of Deitz (1969), Dentler and Monroe (1961),
Duncan (1978), Gold (1963), Hirschi (1971), Miller and Simon (1974), Riege (1972), Schoenberg (1975), Slocum and
Stone (1963), Zucker (1943).

The Johnson study (1979) referred to earlier, based
on 734 self-administered questionnaires completed by Seattle high school sophomores, by contrast, produced only
slim evidence of a causal role for affective ties to parents
in generating delinquent behavior (pp. 104–105). Most of
the studies that yielded evidence of significant differences
on the affection-acceptance dimension had been relying
on groups whose delinquent or nondelinquent behavior
could be behaviorally more sharply defined than the Johnson subjects.

Family Relationships

The nature of family relationships is another family
functioning variable that has been explored extensively for
its possible association with delinquent behavior. The
Gluecks (1950) reported that one-third of their delinquent
sample came from homes with spousal conflict, compared
to 15 percent of the nondelinquent population. Nye (1973)

found a significant association between juvenile delinquency of girls and quarreling as well as arguing parents.
For boys no similar clear-cut relationship could be established (pp. 48–50). Quarrelsome, neglectful homes were
found by McCord and McCord (1964) to be especially likely
to produce delinquent boys (70 percent versus 30 percent
in harmonious homes). The Grogans (1968), reviewing
others' research, concluded that inordinate intrafamilial
conflict and tension seem to be a primary contributing factor to delinquent behavior.

In recent years researchers have paid special attention
to the parent-child conflict, particularly because of widespread societal concern about child abuse and neglect. Carr,
Gelles, and Hargreaves (1978), after examining data in
eight New York counties, concluded that "certain types of
family environments are conducive to children being mal-
treated and becoming delinquent" (pp. 26–27). Alfaro
(1978) found child abuse and neglect related to later socially deviant behavior. Four decades earlier, Healy and
Bronner (1936) had found that delinquent children differed from nondelinquent children mainly in the nature
of the relationship in which the children were thwarted
and rejected (p. 77). The research mentioned under the
heading of "Parental Affection/Acceptance" has a bearing
on the present category of variables associated with juvenile
delinquency because lack of such affection or acceptance
may border on conflict or signify other deficiencies in family relationships. At least one study of Israeli middle-class
juvenile delinquents did not support the parent-child conflict thesis: Rahav (1976) found that level of conflict or
consensus between the boy and his parents was not significantly correlated with juvenile delinquency. The author
suggests that "in Israel the conflicts and stresses resulting
from social change and culture conflict overshadow the
troubled family as causes of delinquency" (p. 268). In line
with the bulk of the studies reported, Langner et al. (1979)

found the two family dimensions, parental coldness and mother excitable-rejecting, predictive of children's aggressive disorders (p. 150).

Slocum and Stone (1963), looking beyond conflict and tension among family members, found that highly democratic homes characterized by a high degree of cooperation and fairness of discipline were less likely to contain children showing delinquency-type behavior (violating certain conventions and standards and/or laws) than families with a less democratic home atmosphere.

Nye (1973) did not conceptualize family relationships in any comprehensive manner, but he found the attitudes of both boys and girls toward both parents significantly related to delinquent behavior (p. 119). Similarly related were their attitudes toward parental discipline, feeling of being accepted by the parent and the marital adjustment of the parents (p. 124). Additionally, agreement between parents and children on a series of value propositions was for the most part negatively related to juvenile delinquency.

The McCords (1964), after subjecting the data of the well-known Cambridge-Somerville study to secondary analysis, concluded that attitudes of both parents toward the child were related to his delinquency and criminal conduct (p. 181).

Hirschi (1969, p. 91) was able to show a connection between self-reported delinquency and intimacy of communication, and it was not simply the frequency but the nature of communication that differentiated between delinquents and nondelinquents. Among more recent investigators into the subject of delinquency and family relationships, Norland, Shover, Thornton, and James (1979) were able to show that family conflict may lead to delinquency when children are alienated from parents or when it results in ineffectual parental control resulting ultimately in juvenile delinquency.

Although the concept "family relations" or "relationships" is used in titles and in the body of books and articles of a number of investigators, few of them take great pains to operationalize or even to define the concept. Their tendency is instead to select terms such as conflict, value disagreement, communication, and the like as an index, the link with family relations remaining undefined.

Parental Supervision/Discipline

Poor parental supervision and inconsistent discipline are variables on which delinquency researchers have focused for at least three decades (Akers, Krohn, Lanza-Kaduce, & Radosevich, 1979; Craig & Glick, 1963; Glueck & Glueck, 1950, 1968; McCord, 1979; McCord et al., 1959; Nye, 1973; Slocum & Stone, 1963; Sterne, 1964; West & Farrington, 1973).

Focusing selectively on some of the specific findings, the Gluecks reported in their 1950 study that lax and inconsistent techniques were more closely associated with delinquency than were strict discipline. Nondelinquent behavior, by contrast, was found to be related to firm but kind disciplinary measures. Physical punishment was used more frequently by parents of delinquents than parents of nondelinquents.

McCord et al. (1959) concluded in their studies that consistency had a greater impact on children's behavior than type of discipline. Consistent love-oriented behavior by both parents was less conducive to delinquency than inconsistent discipline. There was a tendency for delinquent boys to be parented by passive, ineffectual mothers. Passive ineffectual fathers were not associated with delinquency if the mother's discipline and supervision were effective.

Nye (1973) analyzed specific disciplinary techniques and found that the disciplinary role of the father is more closely related to delinquent behavior than is that of the mother (p. 90). Slocum and Stone (1963) reported a significant relationship between fairness of parental discipline and conforming male and female children.

West and Farrington (1973) found very strict or erratic discipline to be associated with delinquent behavior. Akers et al. (1979) in a recent study found a curvilinear relationship between parental disciplinary actions (either harsh or ignoring) and adolescents' use and abuse of alcohol and marijuana; and Hirschi (1971), investigating the effect of parental supervision on the behavior of the child, reported that "children who perceive their parents as unaware of their whereabouts are highly likely to have committed delinquent acts" (p. 89).

Family Deviance and Disorganization

This category of family functioning comprises forms of behavior that are clearly at odds with accepted standards and are likely to violate some existing laws as well. There is some inevitable overlapping with the three preceding conceptual headings in that behavior at the negative end of each continuum (acceptance versus rejection, relationships good versus conflict, supervision adequate versus none) may in the extreme case represent a form of deviant behavior. Deviance as used here denotes behavior that is proscribed and calls for intervention as is the case with parental criminality and child abuse.

The Gluecks, utilizing data of their 1950 study *Unraveling Juvenile Delinquency* (the sample was composed of 500 white delinquent and 500 white nondelinquent boys matched by residence in underprivileged areas, age, ethnic origin, and global intelligence), concluded that "the families of the delinquents' parents were more extensively characterized than those of the non-delinquents by mental retardation, emotional disturbance, drunkenness, and criminalism" (Glueck & Glueck, 1968, p. 16). The immediate families of the delinquents were headed by fathers with a lesser capacity to earn an honest living, who gave less adequate oversight to the children, and who maintained weaker family ties. Delinquents' families more often than those of nondelinquents were headed by parents who were indifferent or hostile toward their children and more erratic or inconsistent (e.g., father punitive, mother permissive) in their child-rearing practices (p. 16). A more tense home atmosphere in families of delinquents as compared to those of non-delinquents is reported by Andry (1971), who also found that the fathers tend to contribute substantially to the existence of such an atmosphere (p. 128). Intrafamilial conflict or deficient relationships were identified as correlates of delinquency by Venezia (1968) and Norland et al. (1979).

Rutter and Madge (1976, p. 169), in their reviews of the research, note that early studies in Britain (Carr-Saunders, Mannheim, & Rhodes, 1942; Ferguson, 1952), in Sweden and Denmark (Hutchings & Mednick, 1974; Otterstrom, 1946), and in the United States (Glueck and Glueck, 1950) all produced similar findings—an increase in the probability of delinquency for boys who have criminal parents and/or delinquent siblings.

Two more recent studies, one in Britain (Farrington, Gundry & West, 1975, West, 1969, West & Farrington, 1973) and one in the United States (Robins, West & Herjanic, 1975), further substantiated the relationship between parental deviance and juvenile delinquency. Robins and her associates looked at the delinquent children of more than 200 families in St. Louis. Delinquent behavior in these children was associated with parental arrests in adult life and with parental delinquency when they (the parents) were juveniles. The association was considerably stronger when *both* parents had been criminally involved. West and Farrington's longitudinal study of nearly 400 boys revealed that roughly half of those with criminal fathers became delinquent; less than one-fifth of those with noncriminal fathers did. One particularly interesting finding of the West and Farrington study is that males who became recidivists only in adulthood were likelier to have criminal fathers than those who became recidivist as juveniles. Other variables with a bearing on family organization/ disorganization have received less attention in research efforts. Gold (1963), as did West and Farrington (1973), found that delinquent youths and their parents shared few leisure activities. McCord's (1979) examination of the Cambridge-Somerville data showed that boys whose mothers lack self-confidence were subsequently more likely to be convicted of both personal and property crimes than boys whose mothers possessed self-confidence. West and Farrington (1973) also found an association between low maternal aspirations for a son's job and delinquent behavior, particularly in boys with above average scholastic achievement.

Wahler, Leske, and Rogers (1978) have emphasized the role of outside forces on these family processes. Disorganized family systems do not have normal community ties or communication networks, which seems to limit the ability of the community's code of behavior to alter the youth's behavior.

Langner and his associates (1979), in a multidiscipli-nary, multivariate, longitudinal study, examining both official records and several types of survey-reported data, determined that overall prediction of juvenile delinquency points to the influences of parental behavior, particularly unhappy marriages, the modeling of antisocial behavior, and parental punitive practices (as well as early mentation problems and childhood behaviors).

Parental abuse of children has in recent years come into focus as a seemingly widespread form of family pa-thology. Several researchers have demonstrated an em-pirical relationship between neglect, maltreatment, and abuse of children and the subsequent deviant behavior of the child (Alfaro, 1978; Carr et al., 1978; Chilton & Markle, 1972; Jenkins, 1974). When extreme and inconsistent discipline and poor supervision (see above) are considered together with rejecting, hostile parental attitudes and cruel and neglecting behavior by the heads of families, parental deviance and pathology would appear to be cardinal predisposing variables in delinquent behavior (McCord, 1979; Rutter & Madge, 1976; West & Farrington, 1973).

Jaffe (1969) treated the subject of family deviance from a perspective of value confusion under the traditional sociological heading "anomie" and obtained empirical evidence that juvenile delinquency and family anomie are related. Discrepancies in value systems between parents and parents and children were found to be significantly more characteristic of families with delinquent than with nondelinquent children in a study by Feather and Cross (1975).

The contextual side of the family deviance-delinquency relationship was examined by Johnstone (1978), who argued that the many findings of association between family variables and juvenile deviant behavior are the result of research with homogeneous populations that do not allow the investigator to unravel the complex relationships between family and the larger environment. Self-report studies, isolating the biasing effect of the juvenile justice system and utilizing representative samples of young people (Hirschi, 1971; Nye, 1973) have usually emerged with weaker relationships and have assessed the impact of family variables more cautiously (Johnstone, p. 300).

In his own study using 6,400 households in the Chicago Standard Metropolitan Statistical Area, Johnstone (1978) found that the impact of the family on delinquency rates varies with the quality of the environment. Although families in poverty-stricken areas tend to be more disrupted, the families' role in generating or preventing delinquency is less pronounced there than in higher income areas. Johnstone's explanation is that in deteriorated areas family influence is overshadowed by poverty or disorganization of the neighborhood, whereas in more affluent settings problematic family life may have a stronger direct effect on the juvenile (pp. 311–312). A similar point is made by Rahav (1976), who concluded that in Israel the conflicts and stresses resulting from rapid social change overshadow the family as causes of delinquency.

Family functioning variables as a group seem to be inextricably linked to delinquent behavior. Juvenile delinquency appears to occur disproportionately among children in "unhappy homes" where there is poor communication; marital disharmony; unaccepting, unaffectionate parents; erratic, extreme discipline; marked tension; and pandemic lack of family cohesiveness. One must be cautious about the general conclusions of the research dealing with family functioning variables, which pose some of the same methodological problems as the studies dealing with structural factors (see for example, Hennessy et al., 1978). Only a few were longitudinal. Most were limited by the hypotheses tested or by lack of consideration of various types of delinquents. Related casual variables were often neglected or left uncontrolled. The influence of poverty on family functioning has been largely ignored (Rodman & Grams, 1967, p. 216). Not enough attention has been given to searching for the interaction of variables, and it has been too infrequently asked why most "susceptible" children escape the prediction of delinquent behavior, or why most juveniles who are officially labeled "delinquent" disentangle themselves from the justice system and do not become adult criminals (p. 206).

Robins (1978, p. 621), after reviewing the findings of several longitudinal studies relating childhood antisocial behavior to adult antisocial behavior, has reiterated the need for identifying which children are at highest risk for delinquency in adulthood so that intervention can be most effective. Patterson (1978), as well, has expressed concern that "more molecular levels of family operation must be examined before predictive accuracy (of youthful delinquency) reaches optimal level" (p. 38).

Given the salience of some of the variables that have been associated in the literature with juvenile delinquency, the more straightforward question must be raised: How important is the family in the causation of delinquency, and by implication, in the prevention or avoidance of delinquency? The gist of the research and writing on the subject indicates, of course, that the family is rarely the direct cause although often a contributing influence to juvenile deviance.

Even in urban neighborhoods that are hotbeds of juvenile delinquency the parents do not generally socialize their offspring into a life of crime. Their act is likely to be one of omission rather than commission. They fail to do the things that parents can do to make their children conform to societal laws and mores.

The foregoing literature review highlighted another aspect of family in the causation of delinquency. It is not parental presence or absence or some particularly structural characteristic such as parents' work status that seems to leave its mark on children's behavior but rather what parents do, referred to above as their functioning, that has a noticeable impact on the degree of children's conformity or deviance.

Many of the factors thus associated with juvenile delinquency could be put under the heading of poor parenting. They impact directly on the behavior of the child in the way that child is accepted, socialized, treated, and so forth. Other family factors also related to delinquency, such as marital disharmony and conflict, do not fall under the rubric of parenting, but because they take place in the family setting they are closely correlated with the parenting process.

From a wider theoretical perspective the significance of these family factors can be viewed in the context of social control theory, which has as its basic premise the notion that deviant behavior occurs when an individual's bonds with society are weak or broken. These bonds, according to Hirschi (1971, pp. 16–34), may take several forms: attachment, belief, involvement, and commitment. In actuality bonds to society may comprise one of these factors, all of them, or their combination. They may vary in strength from minimal presence to great potency.

Social control theory is also concerned with the reciprocal object of the bond. Durkheim (1961), for instance, concluded that the three groups that are most important in generating morality are the family, the nation, and humanity (p. 83), although not necessarily in that order (he considered the nation to be particularly important). Delinquency theorists who employ control theory identify also the school, church, and occupational groupings as entities capable of producing bonds. Some control theorists such as Nye (1973, pp. 5–6) include internal as well as external forms of control, the former being exercised through the human conscience.

Social control theory is thus an attempt to explain behavior within its conformity-deviance perspective in terms of the sum total of influences that may produce one or the other. In view of the fact that in modern society there are multiple forces impinging on the young person, some of them (like the police and courts) exercising control not by way of bonds but social restraint, control theory needs to take account of all of them and weigh their contribution in bringing about conformity or deviance.

The family focus of the present volume should be considered a key aspect of social control theory. Putting the family in a focal position when seeking to get at the causes of delinquency does not deny the potential importance of other factors but assumes instead that in modern democratic society the family wields a major influence on the children's behavior. In presenting this argument we follow the reasoning of Nye (1973) who stated that

> the family is considered to be the single factor most important in exercising social control over adolescents. This is not to maintain that it is the only significant group in this respect. Peer groups in neighborhoods, schools, churches, and other formal and informal groups are important, as are certain categories of adults such as teachers, police, ministers, adult friends, and national heroes. (p. 8)

Just as the family is not seen as the only variable affecting young people's behavior but rather the most salient one, so social control theory does not present itself as the perfect explanation for delinquent behavior. Control theory is merely the logically most appropriate framework within which juvenile behavior can be understood as being the result of diverse environmental influences shaping human behavior. There is no presumption of these accounting totally for the delinquency of minors and of discounting the effect of genetic and other biological factors, personality characteristics, or legal administrative structures.

Bahr's (1979) survey of the literature concludes that empirical data appear generally consistent with the basic tenets of social control theory (p. 621). The inventory of family variables associated with juvenile delinquency emphasizes the importance of the family variable in the social control formulation. These observations lead directly to the ultimate question of whether the family occupies a significant place in a theory of causation.

There is no easy answer to this question, given the many direct and indirect ways in which the family may exert its influence on its offspring. Parental roles and attitudes at the time of a child's adolescence are of course readily observable and measurable. Yet their impact may be quite negligible compared to the parental influence, not as easily measured, during the early stages of socialization. Parental impact also might have taken such indirect forms as choice of neighborhood in which to live and selection of schools, clubs, and other bodies contributing to child socialization. Parental influence at any one point in time might also be overshadowed by the effect of peer groups (Feldman, Caplinger, & Wodarsky, 1983).

The survey of family variables presented above indicates that there is at this stage no way of expressing a causal relationship between parental or family factors and juvenile delinquency in precise terms. This lack of precision results from a number of circumstances: (a) The family variables are many, and we have dealt with them under four major headings. A number of them show a significant relationship to juvenile delinquency, but some do not. In a few instances findings seem contradictory (Hirschi, 1971, pp. 83–94; Johnson, 1979, pp. 103–105). (b) Delinquency is defined in a number of ways: officially reported delinquency, school behavior, self-reported delinquent behaviors, probation and placement in training schools, frequency of offense, seriousness of offense, and others. (c) The populations studied vary considerably, and representative samples are the exception, not the rule. (d) Most studies, particularly the early ones, use relatively primitive techniques of data analysis that do not reveal the simultaneous effect of several variables or their interaction. Such studies make only a minor contribution toward a theory of causation.

Theories of delinquency are first and foremost attempts to describe the characteristics as well as regularities of deviant behavior and furnish some explanations about the whys of its occurrence. Such theories have a secondary goal—perhaps of minor importance to the basic researcher but of major significance to the applied behavioral scientist and practitioner—that of pointing the way to a strategy for dealing with the problem at hand. Strategies can be of a remedial or preventive nature depending very much on the nature of the theory and the means available for attacking the problem. Biological theories and psychodynamic ones, locating the problem in heredity and early socialization, respectively, have little bearing on reducing the number of delinquents roaming the streets at the present time. Social control theory, although it may not come to grips with the obstacles created by biogenetic disorders, defects in early child rearing, or the social and economic inequities in modern society, does put the spotlight on the relationship between the potential or actual delinquent and those in his/her environment wielding some influence on the youngster. This theory focuses on what happens at present and offers the possibility of intervention that promises to have an impact on the delinquency problem.

Of all the significant others in the delinquent's life the parents are most accessible and probably most subject to influence from a benign helping agent. It is certainly easier to reach parents than school systems, peer groups, neighborhood organizations, churches, courts, police departments, and so on. There is some good evidence that regardless of social class, parents are concerned about deviant behavior of their children (Hirschi, 1971, pp. 96–97). There is even reason to believe that families who themselves may be involved in illegal activities will still be opposed to the delinquent behavior of their own offspring (Sykes & Matza, 1957, p. 665).

The fact that parents are accessible and very likely interested in doing something to limit the delinquency of their minor children does not mean that existing correctional activities emphasize such an approach. The services and programs in this country that deal with young persons who have been identified as delinquents do not, by and large, seek to involve the family in action aimed at control and rehabilitation. The contemporary juvenile justice system, allowing for some exceptions, focuses on the individual offender. We shall examine this situation more closely in a subsequent chapter.

In summarizing this discussion we reiterate that the formulation advocated here is not presented as a comprehensive theory of juvenile delinquency but as a theoretical framework that has credibility as a result of numerous empirical studies and relevance for social intervention because the causal variables are located within the purview of feasible programs and services.

Chapter 3

FAMILY FUNCTIONING AND THE RESOCIALIZATION OF JUVENILE OFFENDERS

CHARACTERISTIC FAMILY FUNCTIONING PATTERNS IN JUVENILE DELINQUENCY

What is the nature of family life in families of juvenile delinquents? Do juveniles who have been in trouble with the law come from families who are poorer, more conflicted, more disorganized, more abusive, more neglectful, more permissive, and so forth? Chapter 2 furnished some evidence that all of these factors may play a role. Other variables such as anomie or inconsistent behavior may come into play as well. One is tempted to apply here a variant on the aphorism applied to mental illness by saying that families of juvenile delinquents are like normal families except more so. Can it be said, then, that there are characteristic family patterns in juvenile delinquency?

With the focus of this book on family functioning we can narrow the question by asking whether the families of juvenile offenders manifest certain functional patterns that help explain the behavior of the deviant youngster. More specifically, do such families give evidence of inability to carry out socially expected tasks in general or of deficiency in performing specific roles and tasks?

At this point we are able to marshal only beginning data on this subject because the family functioning analysis has not been applied to representative samples of families with delinquent children. Instead the evidence comes from two studies—one Australian, the other done in New Jersey—comprising a total of 82 (60 and 22, respectively) families with a delinquent child who was placed on probation for the first time at the start of the study.

The measurement technique used in the two studies as well as in other family groups shown for comparison is identical. It utilizes the St. Paul Scale in Family Functioning (Geismar, 1980), which assesses the family's performance of socially expected roles in nine areas of social functioning on a seven-point scale whose evaluative dimensions are health-welfare and conformity-deviance. A 60- to 90-minute interview, generally with the mother, and observation of the home environment are entered into a 27-category schedule by the interviewer. This material is then coded in terms of the aforementioned criteria with the aid of a 20-page manual.

The scale has undergone repeated tests for reliability and validity (Geismar, 1980, pp. 168–170). For purposes of the present discussion it is necessary to identify the nine main areas of family functioning shown in Table 3-1. It should be noted that the first four areas are mainly concerned with intrafamilial relationships (family relationships and unity, individual behavior and adjustment, care and training of children, and social activities). The subsequent three areas are predominantly instrumental areas of functioning or activities devoted to maintaining the family as a structural entity that meets the physical needs of its members (economic practices; home and household prac-

Table 3-1.
The Social Functioning Profiles of Families of Juvenile Delinquents and Other Families Compared

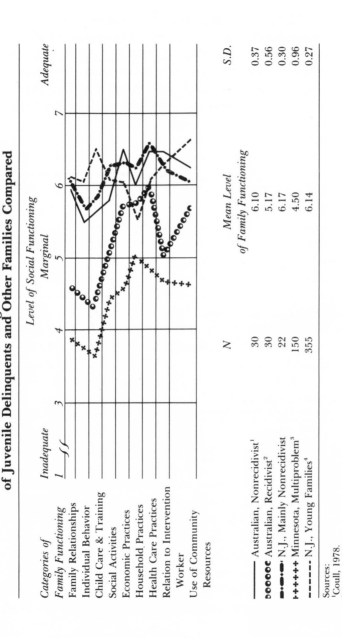

				Mean Level of Family Functioning	S.D.
			N		
Australian, Nonrecidivist[1]			30	6.10	0.37
Australian, Recidivist[2]			30	5.17	0.56
N.J., Mainly Nonrecidivist[2]			22	6.17	0.30
Minnesota, Multiproblem[3]			150	4.50	0.96
N.J., Young Families[4]			355	6.14	0.27

Sources:
[1]Coull, 1978.
[2]Coull, 1978.
[3]Geismar & La Sorte, 1964, pp. 88–89.
[4]Geismar, 1973, p. 46.

tices, and health conditions and practices). The remaining two areas cover extrafamilial relations, mainly relationships to the intervention worker(s), if this is applicable, and to community organizations in the fields of education, religion, health, welfare, and recreation (relationship to intervention worker and use of community resources).

In reading the graphs in Table 3-1 it should be noted that whereas the theoretical range of scores in levels of family functioning is from 1 to 7—and individual families score over the total range in one category or another—the empirical distribution of mean scores of groups of families studied up to this point stretches from about 3.6 to 6.6.

One of the interesting observations arising from the five family functioning graphs is the close similarity between the profiles of New Jersey families of juvenile offenders and the Australian families of nonrecidivist delinquents (for more details, see discussion below). It should be pointed out that the analysis of the Australian study population differentiated between recidivists and nonrecidivists. It should be noted furthermore that these two groups differed strikingly (and statistically significantly). The family functioning graph of New Jersey families was not based on a sorting out of recidivism and nonrecidivism. However, at the halfway mark of the observation period (about 6 months after the youths were put on probation) only 3 out of the 22 New Jersey youngsters had violated the conditions of probation; and the activities logs, used to record the probationers' behavior, did not point toward anything resembling widespread recidivism in this group. In short, the New Jersey graph represents basically a nonrecidivist population, comparable in that regard to the Australian nonrecidivist group. The difference between mean total functioning scores was 0.06 of a scale step, and the mean discrepancy of main category scores amounted to 0.18 of that measure, ranging from 0.08 to 0.36 or about one-third of a scale step. Considering the differences among the various profile graphs shown, the two nonrecidivist family groups show a striking resemblance. Nonetheless, there is need to put the measures into an overall perspective relative to the rest of the data brought together for purposes of comparison. The overall level of social functioning of families with a delinquent child does not vary sharply from a randomly selected group of young American (New Jersey) families residing in a medium-size, problem-ridden city. The general level is comparable in degree of adequacy, but the specific shape of the young families' profile differs in showing somewhat greater adequacy in expressive (intrafamilial relationship) areas and lesser adequacy in instrumental areas. The latter reflects the general socioeconomic conditions of the city as well as problems associated with the early family life cycle when income and housing are in a formative stage.

Particularly noteworthy in the comparison of functioning patterns is the large difference between recidivist and nonrecidivist families. The graphs support visually the statistically very significant differences between the two types of families emerging from the Australian study. Although the slopes of the two graphs are quite similar, they are far apart particularly in intrafamilial relationship areas and in the relationship to the intervention worker (probation officer). The latter is not surprising and indicates that there was considerable trouble in the relationship between the probation officer and his/her charge before he violated the conditions of probation. The pronounced contrasts in intrafamilial functioning point to problems in the way family members related to one another. The similarity in shapes between the two groups of families with children on probation reveals, nonetheless, a common characteristic of greater problems in expressive areas of functioning. This is in contrast to the social functioning pattern of randomly selected young urban families who do not reveal the same slope of lesser expressive adequacy. What is identified here as a potential problem graph among families served by the correctional authority is validated by the shape of the profile representing multiproblem families. The multiplicity of problems in such families, demonstrated in more than one study (Geismar & LaSorte, 1964, p. 88) are concentrated mainly in the inter- and intrapersonal areas of behavior. It is suggested here that while the overall location of the profile graph on the seven-point social functioning continuum is an indication of degree of general deprivation, the relative position of expressive and instrumental categories furnishes a clue to the extent to which the family is integrated or disorganized. Although extent of malfunctioning in any area (Geismar, LaSorte, & Ayres, 1962) serves as a useful index for judging the difficulties the family faces in carrying out socially expected tasks, relatively greater problems in the interpersonal categories would indicate behavioral adjustment problems with a variety of consequences, ranging from the need to use mental health services to being in trouble with the law.

The differences in slope between the graphs of recidivists and nonrecidivist families puts a damper on any notion that there is a typical profile of families with a delinquent offspring. It can at best be said at this point that such families may be characterized by a discrepancy in expressive and instrumental functioning, a characteristic seemingly shared by other families in need of adjustment services. By the same token the contrast between families with one-time and repeat offenders (as far as such information is known during a 6-months to 1-year follow-up period) strongly suggests that families of juvenile offenders differ in their social functioning patterns no less than do delinquents themselves, and that the presence of a repeat offender is significantly correlated with more problematic family functioning, particularly in the intra- and interpersonal domains.

Although correlations, no matter how significant, are not generally prima facie evidence of a causal relationship, the juxtaposition of age of family and offender and timing of offense (first major offense committed in the recent past) suggest, nonetheless, that the flow of influence was mainly—even granting some family upset when the youngster was sentenced to a term of probation—from family functioning that includes behavior as well as interaction to behavior of delinquent son. This follows because the nature of the data collection took into account the mode of family life prior to the youngster's court appearance.

Recidivists, we surmise, are much more likely to belong to families where the level of child care is near marginal, characterized by inconsistent or harsh discipline or lack of supervision or rejection. In such families the marital relationship tends to be a problem. The behavior of the father and the mother is more likely to be disturbed or deviant (Coull, 1978). In the light of this background one might project that the first offense of the recidivist will tend to be the start of a delinquent career nourished by the home environment, whereas the first offense of the nonrecidivist is an act that does not fit the social context of the youngster.

Given the range in levels of social functioning among families with a delinquent child, the common characteristic among the families' profiles thus provides us only with hints regarding types of interpersonal problems. This observation makes it necessary to take a further step and search for additional patterns among families of juvenile offenders.

A reading of the 22 New Jersey cases reveals a gamut of social situations ranging from upper-middle-class affluence at one end to abject poverty at the other.*⟨Not surprisingly, more families were near the poverty end, not only because the communities from which the sample was drawn had a heavy concentration of economically deprived and minority families but also because crime and delinquency are more prevalent among populations characterized by material deprivation. At the bottom of the socioeconomic range are four families receiving public assistance (three of which are headed by single mothers). At the opposite end is a millionaire who owns a chain of businesses. Between these extremes are families headed by blue-collar and lower-level white-collar workers, most of whom are in the employ of others (only three are self-employed) earning incomes close to or below the median of U.S. family incomes ($23,433 in 1982). Of the 18 non-public-assistance families 4 are headed by a single parent. Two of these are the biological mothers, one is a male relative acting as the legal guardian, and the fourth is the youngster's grandmother. Of the two-parent situations three are reconstituted families in which one parent remarried or is living with a paramour and one is the case of the probationer living with the nuclear family of his older brother. That

---

*The socioeconomic distribution of the New Jersey sample was quite similar to the sample of Australian families (Coull, 1978) whose occupational ranking on the seven-point Congalton Status Scale (Congalton, 1969) was concentrated (two-thirds of study group) in the two bottom categories (unskilled and semiskilled). Only 8 percent of the families were headed by persons in middle-class occupations (one being a physician). No significant occupational status differences were found between families whose boys turned recidivist and families with youngsters whose probation sentence was terminated.

leaves a modal group of 10 families (45 percent of sample) headed by two parents and living in the first marriage and 4 families (18 percent of study group) also headed by two parents but not necessarily the natural ones. From the point of view of family structure these families are not very deviant in a society in which in 1978 only 78 percent of noninstitutional children under eighteen lived with two parents (COFO MEMO, Summer/Fall 1979, p. 4). That ratio is even lower for lower-class and racial minority families.

Although the structure of the families of juvenile offenders reveals lower-class traits, and functioning patterns suggest relatively greater malfunctioning in interpersonal and expressive than in instrumental areas, none of these characteristics are unique to families with children who are juvenile offenders. One likely reason for the lack of clear family patterning may be found in the fact that a delinquent act that leads to probation is not necessarily a form of behavior with deep roots in family life (or intrapersonal life for that matter).

In our sample, breaking and entering and incorrigibility were the two offenses accounting for about half of the law violations putting youngsters on probation for the first time. Breaking and entering is generally an activity done in groups, hence a component of the street culture surrounding the family's residence. It is hard to discern from the police record the extent to which the probationer was a leader or follower during the act recorded in the police file. As might be expected, both the probationer and his family claimed almost invariably that the initiative was in the hands of other children. Incorrigibility, the second common juvenile offense, is a poorly defined entity denoting, above all, lack of parental control over their child's behavior, which by itself does not belong in the serious offense category. Among the 22 cases only 2 relatively serious delinquent acts are noted, one of robbery and the second of burglary, suggesting possibly a more deep-seated tendency toward criminal behavior. Other delinquent acts comprised such acts as fighting with a windshield scraper (defined as assault), possession of alcohol and/or marijuana, car theft, and pocketbook snatching. The Australian sample, it should be noted, also revealed a pattern of juvenile offenses with a moderately low level of seriousness (mean values of 2.8 for recidivists and 3.2 for nonrecidivists on a "Seriousness of Offense Scale," in which the lowest values are traffic offenses (1) and other offenses against the good order (2) and the highest ones are robbery (8) and assault (aggravated) (9) (Coull, 1978, p. 122). Both data sets indicate that juvenile delinquent acts leading to probation comprise a considerable variety of behaviors whose origins can be traced to peer group, street environment, family, and of course, personality. Some delinquency, and not an insignificant amount, is mainly the result of society's handling of the case as the labeling theorists have well demonstrated (Krisberg & Austin, 1978, pp. 194–216).

If the diverse nature of probation-related juvenile delinquency and its seemingly multicausal nature make it difficult to correlate with types of family structure and functioning, it does not follow that the family has no role to play in the treatment and rehabilitation of their offspring. The family's role in the rehabilitation of the youngster can be viewed in a long-term as well as a short-term perspective. The former relates to the parent(s)' ability to function as effective socializers who can help their child to achieve a more conforming way of life. This is an ambitious goal and may be beyond the parents' reach, depending on a variety of factors such as the personalities of family members, family relationship patterns, and environmental pressures. The achievement of the long-range goal is likely to be contingent to a large extent on short-term goal attainment. The latter represents a more modest challenge in the form of a collaborative endeavor in which the probation service recruits the family for a partnership that will aid the offender to live within the boundaries of the court order and terminate the status on schedule.

The basis for the collaboration is the common interest—shared by the delinquent, his/her parents, and the probation service—to make probation a one-time, self-liquidating experience within the court-controlled juvenile justice system. Underlying this endeavor, however, is the assumption that a constructive probation experience can open the way toward achieving the longer-range goal of resocializing the delinquent and integrating him/her into the family and community.

SOCIALIZATION AND RESOCIALIZATION

From a social control theory perspective the socialization of children is a key variable influencing the conformity or deviance of the person growing to adulthood. There is an extensive literature on the subject, and as might be expected, the variegated analysis has given rise to numerous definitions ranging from "lengthy and abstract paragraphs to terse statements of human behavior" (Kennedy & Kerber, 1973, p. 4). What all of the definitions appear to have in common is the notion of a process in which an individual, generally a child, acquires knowledge, skills, and habits that enable him or her to participate as a more or less effective member of groups and society (Brim, 1966; Clausen, 1968; Maccoby, 1968).

Resocialization, by contrast, presupposes that an individual has already been socialized but that the previous socialization was found to be deficient relative to the values and norms of society or group to which the individual belongs. In resocialization that individual and/or his environment is then subjected to intervention aimed at bringing about attitudes and behavior consonant with the prevalent norms and values.

In socialization as well as resocialization the acquisition of knowledge, skills, and habits is aimed at enabling the person to function in keeping with prevailing social norms and expectations. Consonance between personal functioning and behavioral norms is usually a prerequisite for effective social participation. Dissonance tends to result in conflict between the individual and the groups and institutions that are the custodians of the norms guiding behavior.

In socialization the primary group, most often the family, is the primary agent, whereas in resocialization secondary groups come into play. We question the assertion by Kennedy and Kerber that the secondary group is *the* primary resocialization agent (1973, p. 45). We believe instead that the role of groups will vary in different socialization processes depending on such factors as the resocializee's age, life cycle stage, and family status, as well as the resocialization tasks faced by him or her. Primary groups are unlikely to play a major role in the life of an adult offender confined to a federal penitentiary and in infrequent contact with family and friends outside the institution. He might, of course, enjoy the support of friendship groups within the prison, but such primary groups will probably not play a resocialization function. By contrast the family, as a primary group, will very likely constitute the primary resocialization agent in the case of an adolescent probationer living at home and attending regular school. Whether the family does or does not do so is, of course, contingent on a variety of other conditions such as the degree of resocialization activity extended by the probation department, neighborhood clubs, peer groups, school counselors, and the likes. It is our thesis that the family is a "natural" resocialization agent, although its potential remains underutilized.

In view of the special focus of this book on the family role in the resocialization of young offenders, one study in which the senior author was a participant merits being cited because it generated data bearing on the above problems. The study, which was conducted in Australia (Coull et al., 1982), compares 30 juvenile recidivists and 30 non-recidivists with regard to the social functioning of their respective families. Social functioning was measured by means of the St. Paul Scale of Family Functioning (Geismar, 1980) in terms of the family's performance of socially expected roles and tasks measured according to criteria of family well-being and conformity-deviance. Resocialization was assessed with the aid of the Family Resocialization Scale, the dimensions of which were parental acceptance versus rejection of probationer, acceptance of a resocialization role, realism versus unrealism toward the offense, and degree of cooperation with the probation agency. Data were obtained by reading case records and interviewing the probation officers who had carried the 60 study cases.

The findings of the Australian researchers need to be presented with one caveat, nevertheless. The data were retrospective. The probation officers had finished serving these children and their families, and the possibility of faulty recollection on subjects that were not recorded cannot be excluded. What mitigates against major distortion is the fact that the probation officers were asked to report on cases that they carried only a short time before the study.

This research was motivated by the hypothesis that the family's influence on the behavior of its children, especially on the extent to which such behavior is conforming or deviant, extends to situations in which the children have already violated the law and been put under court supervision. The sample was comprised of cases put on probation for the first time, and it was thought that since this event represented a time of crisis in the lives of the families, the family would be challenged to react in ways that might have a significant impact on the lives of the children. Positive social functioning as defined by the St. Paul Scale of Family Functioning and a supportive attitude toward the child were expected to be matched by a cooperative disposition toward the probation agency.

The results of the analysis supported the hypothesis more strongly than expected. Ten percent of the children of more adequately functioning families became recidivists within a year, as against 87 percent of those whose families functioned more problematically. Acceptance of the probationer (as against rejection), acceptance of a resocialization role, and cooperation with the probation department were significantly correlated with positive outcome (non-recidivism) denoted by phi coefficients of 0.67, 0.43, and 0.37, respectively. Only one of the measures used, the degree of realism with which the family viewed the offense, bore no significant relationship to probation outcome.

A further analysis of these data showed the positive effects of family life to revolve around the supportive and expressive aspects of social functioning (Coull et al., 1982). Of special interest is the finding that the social functioning of the family at the time their son was put on probation had greater impact on his rehabilitation than the attitudes and activities of the family following court action. From the point of view of control theory, however, such functioning is as easily within the grasp of the researcher-practitioner as are subsequent attitudes and activities. And judging from the data generated in the Australian study there is substantial merit in targeting both as prime objects of rehabilitative intervention.

Chapter 4

FAMILY TREATMENT PROGRAMS
A Balance Sheet

HISTORICAL DEVELOPMENT OF DELINQUENCY REHABILITATION

Institutionalization has traditionally been the primary means utilized in the attempt to rehabilitate juvenile offenders. Over the years, however, its general failure has been well documented. Although some institutionally based behavior modification programs report success in changing the behavior and attitudes of delinquents, the effects seem both to be short-lived and to fail to generalize to the youngster's behavior after he is discharged to his natural world of family, neighborhood, and former companions (Lane & Burchard, 1983).

In 1967 a Task Force Report was issued by the President's Commission on Law Enforcement and Administration of Justice that concluded that the juvenile justice system had failed to rehabilitate delinquents or to deter others from delinquency. Extensive reforms of the system were initiated, including exclusion of minor offenders (cf. Schur, 1973) and development of community-based alternatives to institutionalization.

Some of these community programs have focused on the delinquent individual alone, via such programs as skill training, work experience, group work with natural gangs, and so on. Not all of the results are in concerning the effectiveness of these approaches, particularly of the newer and more innovative variety; but outcome research concerning the more traditional individual and group treatment attempts has indicated that they are *not* effective methods for rehabilitation of the juvenile delinquent (Berleman, Seaberg, & Steinburn, 1972; Craig & Furst, 1965; Lerman, 1970; McCord et al., 1959; Powers & Witmer, 1951; Tait & Hodges, 1972). In fact, some of these programs found *increased* delinquent behavior of their treated groups as compared to the cases that had not received professional treatment. Regardless of the particular therapeutic approaches utilized or their theoretical underpinnings, all of these approaches have been characterized by a focus on the juvenile himself as "the client."

The history of treatment of delinquency does, however, demonstrate cyclical attention to inclusion of the family as a hypothesized etiological factor and/or as a resource in the attempt at rehabilitation of the young offender. As mentioned in Chapter 2, early studies and crudely empirical formulations as to the nature and etiology of juvenile delinquency tended to emphasize such family variables as "the broken home," "working mothers," and "father-absence" as causative in the generation of adolescent delinquent behavior (Glueck and Glueck, 1950, 1957, 1962, 1968). Because theoretical understanding of the complexity of the family and development of intervention technologies were at an even less sophisticated level than obtains today, earlier attempts at intervention that included the family tended to be exhortatory in technique and undirected by any more than the practitioner's instincts and middle-class perspective on how a family should function.*

The years that followed the end of World War II saw an almost complete dominance of the intervention armamentarium of the helping professions by the psychoanalytically derived focus on the intrapsychic life of the individual. Treatment was therefore almost invariably undertaken in the format of the individual interview. Even when the parents (but most frequently only the mother) were involved in the treatment of a child or adolescent "Identified Patient," they were usually seen in separate psychotherapy focused on their own presumed psychopathology.

In the early 1950s a number of mental health practitioners (mostly psychoanalytically trained), many of whom were working with institutionalized schizophrenics, became intrigued by their observation that the patient's psychotic symptoms seemed to recrudesce when he was visited by his family. Sometimes the observers wondered who was "sicker," the patient or his family members; and the patient's psychosis began to be seen as, at least in part, a comprehensible reaction to a "crazy" family situation. These practitioners then began to move away, ideologically, from their exclusive focus on the individual; and by the 1960s a family therapy "movement" had begun to emerge, focused on the family system as the "patient" rather than on the symptomatic member (Brodkin, 1980).

Although most interventions are still focused on the delinquent himself, increasingly treatment programs can be located somewhere on a continuum ranging from, at minimum, a consideration that the youngster's family has an influence on him (although he is still defined as "owning"

*See, for example, Robins (1966) for an account of child guidance clinic practice before World War II.

his pathology) to a perspective at the other pole that the delinquent's behavior reflects not "internalized intrapsychic pathology" at all, nor even the influence of extrafamily forces, but is invariably and always only the expression of a pathological state of the family system.

Still others conclude, however, that although family may be one variable in delinquency, other antecedent and intervening variables such as socioeconomic class, community and neighborhood characteristics, and the orientation and influence of the youngster's peer group are more powerful determinants. What emerges from the enormous and enormously inconsistent body of literature is that the family's role as a variable in the etiology or in the prevention of delinquency represents neither a linear relationship nor one uncontaminated by the influence of other factors. However, the family does appear to play some role, and it is "still the most salient social system available to aid in the prevention of further antisocial behavior" (Byles & Maurice, 1979).

Family therapists who subscribe to a "systems" perspective hypothesize that some dysfunction in the network of relationships, rewards, sanctions, power distribution, communication channels and processes, and exchange of information and emotion that characterizes the internal world of the family system has brought about and/or is perpetuating the behavior of its delinquent youngster. Family-oriented clinicians with a behaviorist perspective seem to be referring to at least a part of the same hypothesized phenomenon when they speak of a system of reciprocal reinforcements within the family that is (usually unwittingly, except in the case of the "criminal" family that actively promulgates antisocial norms) creating or perpetuating the antisocial behavior of its son or daughter.

The family therapy perspective, the development of behavior modification theory and techniques, and the movement of delinquency treatment out of the institution have intersected in time with the search for community-based rehabilitative approaches to the young offender. Concurrently, however, question has been raised by such critics as Illich (1976), Lasch (1977), Platt (1977), and Rothman (1978) as to the capacity of currently constituted social agencies to be of effective help to families. Famiglietti (1981) summarizes this critical literature as charging that professionals "in their zeal to alleviate the glaring needs of dependent groups such as juvenile offenders, have assumed in the name of the state the role of parent and have instituted reforms and programs that have often been coercive and intrusive" and that have "undermined the confidence and capability of families to solve their own problems" (p. 4). Since the empirical evidence has long been clear that most juvenile delinquents do "grow out of" their adolescent trouble making without treatment of any kind, an additional critical issue is that of identifying those delinquents for whom this normal process will not occur and who do need professional intervention.

Review of the historical development of delinquency rehabilitation seems to indicate clearly that much work remains in the formulation of more effective approaches to the problem. Our next step is the examination of existing evidence regarding the effectiveness of family involvement in the rehabilitation process.

THE RESEARCH EVIDENCE

A diligent effort, including a computer search, was undertaken to locate as many published studies of family treatment of delinquency as possible. Although we cannot claim that no study has gone unnoticed, those reported in Tables 4-1 and 4-2 do represent at least the great majority of empirical research through 1983 that was reported in the professional literature on the effect of family-oriented treatment of delinquency.

Clinical research on delinquency that includes the family in intervention efforts can, for clarity of exposition, be roughly divided into behavioral and nonbehavioral therapeutic approaches, although increasingly these perspectives are being used in conjunction with one another. Table 4-1 (pp. 58–83) summarizes 30 studies of the effect of behavioral interventions with delinquents in which the family was included. Table 4-2 (pp. 98–136) summarizes 21 studies of interventions with delinquents and their families in which the theory and techniques utilized were from other than a behavioral perspective.

The rating system of the adequacy of the research designs and executions ("high credibility," "some limitations," or "inconclusive evidence") is adapted from the schema developed by Gurman and Kniskern (1978, pp. 820–821), encompassing a variety of commonly accepted criteria of adequacy for experimental research. The judgment of adequacy was based on, for example, whether the assignment to the treatment condition(s) was controlled; whether an adequate control or comparison group was used or, in the case of single-organism designs, such devices as multiple baselines; whether the assignment to experimental or control/comparison conditions was unbiased; whether change was measured before and after intervention; whether or not the major independent variable (the intervention) was contaminated by multiple treatments, multiple therapists, or relative therapist competencies; whether or not an appropriate follow-up time period was permitted to elapse before gathering data on such indices of change relevant to delinquency as recidivism rates; whether multiple vantage points for assessing data and multiple change indices were utilized; whether outcome was assessed in terms of change of family relationships as well as change in the individual "I.P." (Identified [delinquent] Patient)—particularly relevant for treatment oriented to family change; whether there is evidence of concurrent treatment or, if such other treatment was received along with the experimental therapy, of its equivalence across groups; whether nonspecific treatment effects (e.g., the "placebo/attention" effect) were controlled for; whether attention was paid to threats to the objectivity of the outcome data (e.g., whether therapists or others with a stake in the treatment outcome were the data gatherers/analysts); whether appropriate statistical analyses were conducted.

Five faculty members who teach research at the Master's or Ph.D. level at the Rutgers University Graduate School of Social Work were asked to rate three studies which, in our judgment, fell into the "high credibility," "some limitations," and "inconclusive evidence" categories utilized in Tables 4-1 and 4-2. The raters, who worked independently of the authors and of each other, rated the studies on a 10-point scale according to the same criteria used in our analysis. The low end of the scale reflected a judgment that the study represented "inconclusive evidence," the midrange represented "some limitations," and the upper range described a study of "high credibility." Individual raters varied no more than one or two points on the scale, and there was unanimous agreement among the raters and between them and the authors on the category assigned to each study. Because the independent raters were able to review only a small sample of the total studies, this can be considered only a partial reliability check on our judgment, but it does offer some evidence that criteria of methodological soundness can be applied to a research study in an objective and consistent fashion.

A caveat should be noted here: some of the research reports reviewed include cases of younger children as well as those in the teen years. There may be reason to believe that empirically supported effectiveness of family treatment

Table 4-1. Studies of Behavioral Family Intervention*

Author	Research Adequacy	Sex-Age-Referral	Methodology	Exp'l N	Control/Comparison	Measures	Data Unbiased?	Follow-up	Outcome Findings
Alexander & Parsons (1973); Klein, Alexander, & Parsons (1977)	High Credibility. But cases followed at only 6 mos may not yet have demonstrated recidivism; failures not explored; instability of exp'l variable (different techniques with different families); N of control group small (additional 4 cases refused testing); no in-	–Male & female; –13–16; –Status offenders referred by court	–Compared exp'l treatment of parent-child behavioral contracting plus communication skills training, with 2 alternate treatments and no-treatment control; –Average 12–15 sessions (but considerable variation). Alternate	N = 46	*Random*; Comparison #1: 19 families in "client-centered" family therapy; Comparison #2: 11 families in "eclectic" family therapy; Control: 6 families no treatment (additional 4 cases refused testing)	–Post-test only: 4 measures of family conflict-resolution skills (audiotaped); –Offense recidivism	Yes (independent raters); Yes	6–18 mos	–E signif. superior on family measures; –E 26% recidivism; no treatment, 50%; client-centered, 47%; family therapy, 73%

		–Sibling court contact	Yes	2½–3½ yrs	–E 20% subsequent court contact siblings vs. 40% no-treatment, 59% client-centered, 63% family therapy
formation given on 15% attrition; no control non-specific treatment effects	treatments also 12–15 sessions (no information re possible variations) –E group therapists graduate students in psychology, received training and supervision				

*Abbreviations used:

C: control or contrast group of cases; the group that does *not* receive the experimental treatment

E: experimental group of cases that *does* receive the experimental treatment

Exp'l: experimental

IP: "Identified Patient"; in these studies, the acting-out adolescent

N: number of cases (in experimental, control, or contrast groups)

(continued)

Table 4-1. Studies of Behavioral Family Intervention* (Continued)

Author	Research Adequacy	Sex-Age-Referral	Methodology	Exp'l N	Control/Comparison	Measures	Data Un-biased?	Follow-up?	Outcome Findings
	High Credibility				*Random*				
Alexander, Barton, Schiavo, & Parsons (1976)	But no follow-up; no control nonspecific treatment effects; no control group	–Male & female –13–16 –Referred by court and social agencies	–Studied effect on case outcome of therapist "relationship" & "structuring" skills –21 therapists of varied experience –Treatment conjoint, focus on modifying communication & problem solving	N = 21	None	–Dropout vs. continuance	Therapists' case outcomes predicted before case assignment by supervisor and project intern (high inter-judge agreement)	None	–9 dropout (43%); relationship skills therapist = 45% variance; structuring skills = 36% variance.

of parents & adolescents			
–Family communication and problem solving (audiotaped)	Yes (independent raters)		–7 (33%) much improved according to family & therapist judgment; 5 (24%) some improvement –Improved cases positive change on family measure.
–Offense recidivism of IP	Yes	12–15 mo	–No recidivism in treated cases vs. 50–60% in dropout group
–Family judgment	No		
–Therapist judgment	No		

(continued)

Abbreviations used:

C: control or contrast group of cases; the group that does *not* receive the experimental treatment

E: experimental group of cases that *does* receive the experimental treatment

Exp'l: experimental

IP: "Identified Patient"; in these studies, the acting-out adolescent

N: number of cases (in experimental, control, or contrast groups)

Table 4-1. Studies of Behavioral Family Intervention* (Continued)

Author	Research Adequacy	Sex-Age-Referral	Methodology	Expl'l N	Control Comparison	Measures	Data Unbiased?	Follow-up	Outcome Findings
Jayaratne (1978)	High Credibility But no control nonspecific treatment effects; data possibly biased by test practice effect; no information re therapists or treatment length; unclear from data if there were failures.	–Male & female –Age "Jr. H.S." –Referred for behavior and academic problems	–Behavioral contracting re family, interruptions, talk time, and decision-making time	N = 13 (both pre- & post-test)	Random N = 15 (post-test only)	–Family interaction in vignette exercises (audio-taped)	Yes (independent raters)	4 mo	–E: decrease interruptions and decision time; no change dominance (talk time)

	High Credibility			Random					
Parsons & Alexander (1973)	Excellent research design but no follow-up; unclear from data if there were failures	−Male & female −X̄ age, 15.3 yr −Referred by court	−Training in negotiation and communication skills, home token economy −Therapists graduate students, 3 wk training −2 sessions/wk for 4 wk; same length for attention/placebo control group	E #1: 10 (both pre- & post-test) E #2: 10 (post-test only)	Control #1: 10 (both pre- & post-test) Control # 2: Attention/placebo (post-test only)	− 4 measures of family communication patterns; measure of family agreement (audiotaped)	Yes (independent raters)	None	−E. significantly improved on family communication; no change on family agreement

(continued)

Abbreviations used:

C: control or contrast group of cases; the group that does *not* receive the experimental treatment

E: experimental group of cases that *does* receive the experimental treatment

Expl: experimental

IP: "Identified Patient"; in these studies, the acting-out adolescent

N: number of cases (in experimental, control, or contrast groups)

Table 4-1. Studies of Behavioral Family Intervention* (Continued)

Author	Research Adequacy	Sex-Age-Referral	Methodology	Expl N	Control/ Comparison	Measures	Data Un-biased?	Follow-up	Outcome Findings
	High Credibility				*Matched*				
Patterson (1974)	Differential effects of various components of treatment package cannot be ascertained (but further research planned on this); E cases had wide range of problem behavior from mild to severe; no control nonspecific treatment effects (but see Walter & Gilmore study which did control for this with same type of treatment); high attrition.	–Male –Presume some adolescents –Referred by court, school, social agencies for "conduct problem"	–Training of parents in behavior management of child, individually and in groups; 31.5 hours professional time. –14 cases also treated in classroom; 28.6 hours professional time –5 experienced therapists, 6 trainees	N = 27 consecutive referrals (10 dropout)	N = 27 "normal" families with nonproblematic child	–Observation family interaction in home and child behavior in classroom –Parents' reports	Yes (independent raters) No	12 mo	–Significant decrease in targeted behaviors to "normal" level of control children –No generalization, as hypothesized, to nontargeted behaviors –Significant improvement in classroom behavior

	High Credibility		Selected from wider sample					
Reid & Hendricks (1973)	–Male –5–14; $\overline{X}$ 8	–Sample of boys who steal *vs.* boys with nonstealing aggressive behavior, from other studies of Patterson et al.	N = 14 stealers	Contrast: N = 11 nonstealers Control: N = 27 nonproblematic families	–Observation family interaction in home	Yes (independent raters)	12 mo	–Treatment twice as effective for nonstealers as for stealers –"Negative coercive behavior" highest in families of nonstealers, next stealers, lowest in normals. –Least positive family interaction in stealer group.

Abbreviations used:

C: control or contrast group of cases; the group that does *not* receive the experimental treatment
E: experimental group of cases that *does* receive the experimental treatment
Exp'l: experimental
IP: "Identified Patient"; in these studies, the acting-out adolescent
N: number of cases (in experimental, control, or contrast groups)

(continued)

Table 4-1. Studies of Behavioral Family Intervention* (Continued)

Author	Research Adequacy	Sex-Age-Referral	Methodology	Exp'l N	Control/Comparison	Measures	Data Unbiased?	Follow-up	Outcome Findings
Robin, Kent, O'Leary, Foster, & Prinz (1977); Robin (1983)	High Credibility But unclear why fathers not involved; no follow-up: low-up: no control nonspecific treatment effects; unclear if there were failures.	-Male & female -11–14 -Mothers & children only -Referred for parent-child conflict	-"PSCT": problem solving communication skills training -Therapists 3 doctoral students; no information re training -5 sessions	N = 12	Random N = 9 wait list (+ 3 dropout)	-Self reports of home conflicts -Audiotaped mother-child problem solving and communication	No Yes (independent raters)	None	-E. significantly improved on office-audiotaped communication skills; no change in home behavior according to self-report questionnaires
Robin (1981, 1983)	High Credibility But only 60% of original sample completed follow-up; no control nonspecific treatment effects; unclear if there were failures; follow-up	-Male & female -11–16, X̄ 14 yrs -Recruited; parent-child conflict	-"PSCT": problem-solving communication training plus cognitive restructuring and generalization programming (homework)	N = 11 (post-data on 6)	Random Contrast: 11 families in "melange" of nonbehavioral family therapy (post-data on 8) Control: 11 wait list	-Family problem solving and communication skills (audiotaped) -Self-reports of home con-	Yes (independent raters) No	8–10 wks	-E superior to both family therapy and control on problem solving and communication and self-report

	–Therapists 1 Ph.D., 3 M.A. psychologists, 1.8 yrs experience vs. 5.7 yrs experience for contrast group family therapists (1 psychiatrist, 3 master's-level professionals). Exp'l therapists received training	–Family therapy slight improvement communication but not problem solving
		–Control worse or no change both measures
	7 sessions both treatments	–Self-reports: change maintained at follow-up

(continued)

Abbreviations used:
C: control or contrast group of cases; the group that does *not* receive the experimental treatment
E: experimental group of cases that *does* receive the experimental treatment
Exp'l: experimental
IP: "Identified Patient"; in these studies, the acting-out adolescent
N: number of cases (in experimental, control, or contrast groups)

67

Table 4-1. Studies of Behavioral Family Intervention* (Continued)

Author	Research Adequacy	Sex-Age-Referral	Methodology	Exp'l N	Control/Comparison	Measures	Data Unbiased?	Follow-up	Outcome Findings
	High Credibility				*Random*				
Shostak (1977)	But not clear why follow-up time so variable; finding of no difference between IOBT; (individual oriented behavioral therapy) and control group might be considered partial control of nonspecific treatment effects; could have been strengthened by use of attention/placebo group; E failures not explored; recidi-	—Male & female —12-17 —Ref. by court & other agencies as delinquent	—"FOBT": (Family Oriented Behavioral Therapy) in Alexander et al. model (q.v.). —Therapists 11 predoctoral students psychology or counseling; previous training —Maximum 8 sessions both treatments; $\overline{X}$ 6.75 FOBT, 5.75 IOBT	N = 8	Contrast: N = 8 in "IOBT": Individual-Oriented Behavior Therapy for IP only Control: N = 8 wait list	—Self-report emotional state —Parents' & IPs' reports problem behaviors of each other —Family interaction (audiotaped) —Family satisfaction with therapist —Therapist judgment	No No Yes (independent raters) Yes No		—Mixed findings on process measures but generally better for FOBT; IOBT no better than no treatment.

Study	Sample	Treatment	Design	Measures	Blind/Follow-up	Follow-up Time	Results
	vism may not have occurred after only 6 wks *Some Limitations* –N is small; no control nonspecific treatment effects; follow-up unclear			–Recidivism	Yes (court & probation blind re exp'l condition)	6 wks to 13 mos	–Recidivism: FOBT, 25%; IOBT, 88%; control, 75%
Kifer, Lewis, Green, & Phillips (1974)	–Male & female –13–17 –Previous court contact –Only 1 parent involved (2 mothers, 1 father)	–Negotiation and communication skills training of parent-child pairs –2 therapists: 1 graduate student; credentials of other not given –9–10 hrs of treatment	*Not Random* 3 N = 1 studies No control group, but multiple baseline across parent-child pairs	–Negotiation behaviors in session and at home	Yes (independent raters)	"An appropriate time period" after termination	–Improvement treated families

Abbreviations used:
C: control or contrast group of cases; the group that does *not* receive the experimental treatment
E: experimental group of cases that *does* receive the experimental treatment
Exp'l: experimental
IP: "Identified Patient"; in these studies, the acting-out adolescent
N: number of cases (in experimental, control, or contrast groups)

Table 4-1. Studies of Behavioral Family Intervention* (Continued)

Author	Research Adequacy *Some Limitations*	Sex-Age-Referral	Methodology	Exp'l N	Control/Comparison	Measures	Data Un-biased?	Follow-up	Outcome Findings
Klees (1979)	Lack of control group not inappropriate for multiple-baseline single-subject design; but follow-up period too brief to measure recidivism; no control nonspecific treatment effects	–Male –15–17 –Referred as chronic delinquent (at least 3 court appearances) –Single-parent families only	–Alexander et al. systems-behavioral treatment (q.v.) –Therapist: author (Ph.D. candidate); previous training various therapies –10 sessions; families paid $100 if all sessions attended	5 (plus 4 dropouts)	None (5 N = 1 studies; multiple-baseline across subjects)	–Family communication in sessions (audiotaped) –"Defensive communication" scale 3/week –Family satisfaction with treatment –Recidivism	Yes (independent raters) ? No Yes	3 mos	–Mixed findings re increased "supportive communication"; no change in "defensive communication"; families satisfied with treatment; –Recidivism 1 case out of the 5 who completed treatment program (but charges dropped because of involvement in

70

Study	Limitations	Sex	Age	Description	Treatment	Random	N	Control	Observation	Independent raters	Follow-up	Results
Patterson, Cobb & Ray (1973)	No control group; no random selection, although cases were consecutive; high attrition; no control nonspecific treatment effects	—Male	—6–13	—Referred by social agencies for "extreme aggressive or acting-out behavior"	—Training family in negotiation skills, parents in behavior management of child, individually and in parents' groups —3–4 mos —2 Ph.D. therapists, 7 trainees	Not Random	N = 13 consecutive referrals (plus 4 drop-out, and full follow-up data available on only 7 cases)	None	—Observation in home of family interaction —Parent records of child's target behaviors	Yes (independent raters) No	12 mos but data at 5 mos for only 9 cases = 15% attrition; for 12 mos on only 7 cases = total attrition 46%	—At termination, target behaviors for all cases as a group decreased 47% from baseline (statistically significant) —No generalization to other behaviors of IP —At 12 mos follow-up, behaviors lower than baseline all 7 cases —2 cases appear to have been clear failures

Abbreviations used:

C: control or contrast group of cases; the group that does *not* receive the experimental treatment

E: experimental group of cases that *does* receive the experimental treatment

Exp'l: experimental

IP: "Identified Patient"; in these studies, the acting-out adolescent

N: number of cases (in experimental, control, or contrast groups)

(continued)

Table 4-1. Studies of Behavioral Family Intervention* (Continued)

Author	Research Adequacy — Some Limitations	Sex-Age-Referral	Methodology	Exp'l N — Not Random to E or C groups	Control/Comparison	Measures	Data Unbiased?	Follow-up	Outcome Findings
Stuart & Lott (1972) Stuart & Tripodi (1973)	Service refusers inadequate control or comparison group: no control nonspecific treatment effects; data not unbiased; no follow-up in this phase of project; no information on treatment dropouts; failures not explored; instability of exp'l variable (influenced by therapist characteristics)	-Male & female -12–15 + -Referred as predelinquent and delinquent	-Study of relative effect varying treatment lengths: E#1: 15 days (6 hours) E#2: 45 days (18 hours) E#3: 90 days (36 hours) -Contingency contracting parents and IP, and with 2 of IP's teachers -Therapists 5 social work students, 1 medical student, 4 professional	N = 79 (random assign. to: E#1 = 26 E#2 = 27 E#3 = 26 (+ some treatment dropouts, but no data given)	Contrast = 15 families who refused treatment	-Court records -Teacher ratings and school grades -Parent ratings of IP behavior -Attitudes of IP -Attitudes of parents	Yes No No No No	None (planned for future phase of project)	-Not enough court appearances to utilize as outcome measure -No major differences according to length of treatment -School attendance and grades significantly worse for untreated group, but also deteriorated for E group

72

social workers; received training

- –Parent ratings and parent attitudes some improvement

- –E group deteriorated in 12 of 30 pre-post comparisons

- –Variability in outcome among therapists

C: control or contrast group of cases; the group that does *not* receive the experimental treatment

E: experimental group of cases that *does* receive the experimental treatment

Exp'l: experimental

IP: "Identified Patient"; in these studies, the acting-out adolescent

N: number of cases (in experimental, control, or contrast groups)

(continued)

Table 4-1. Studies of Behavioral Family Intervention* (Continued)

Author	Research Adequacy	Sex-Age-Referral	Methodology	Exp'l N	Control/Comparison	Measures	Data Un-biased?	Follow-up	Outcome Findings
	Some Limitations				*Random*				
Stuart, Jayaratne, & Tripodi (1976)	Withdrawal of troubled youths from C but not from E group does not bias in favor of E group; but half of C cases received one or more of exp'l interventions (from teachers), compromising placebo-only control condition; evaluatory outcome measures not unbiased; no follow-up	–Male & female –12–15 + –Referred by schools for academic and behavior problems	–Behavioral contracting between parent-child and child-teachers –Some received tutoring –2 inexperienced, 1 experienced MSW social workers, 2 Ph.D. psychology candidates, 9 hours with family, 5.75 hours with teachers professional time –Max., 4 mos	N = 22 (+ 8 on whom posttest data not available)	N = 25 Activity group placebo control (+ 5 dropped by school project from C group as needing actual treatment elsewhere) –1 hour with youth in group, 1.15 hours with teacher professional time –13 C cases also received behavioral contracting, teachers' daily ratings, and/or tutoring	–Parents' evaluation of home and school behavior –Teachers' daily ratings of academic performance and behavior –School grades –School absences –Evaluations of school behavior by school counselor –Court contacts	No No (only 0.25 correlation with report card grades) Yes No Yes	None	–Significant improvement E group on only 4 measures (evaluations by teachers, school counselors, mothers); no significant difference on 9 other measures –3.3% E court contacts vs. 6.7% for C group

74

	Some Limitations			Random						
Stuart, Tripodi, Jayaratne, & Camburn (1976)	–Outcome measures not unbiased (teachers' evaluations particularly showed poor correlation with school grades later assigned); no information given re how many C group subjects received other help elsewhere; no follow-up	–Male & female 12–15+ –Referred by school for academic and behavior problems	–Behavioral contracting between parent-child and child-teachers –No information on therapists; 20.57 hours professional time; 4 mos	N= 57	N= 45 refused treatment by therapists; given option of seeking help elsewhere	–Parents' evaluation of home and school behavior –Teachers' daily ratings and principal's evaluation of school behavior –School grades –School absences	No No (only 0.25 correlation with report card grades) Yes	None	–E group "small but statistically significant improvement" on 5 of 10 measures (evaluations of school behavior by teachers, principals, and parents; reports of improved interaction with mother)

(continued)

75

Table 4-1. Studies of Behavioral Family Intervention* (Continued)

Author	Research Adequacy	Sex-Age-Referral	Methodology	Exp'l N	Control/ Comparison	Measures	Data Un-biased?	Follow-up	Outcome Findings
Stuart, Tripodi, Jayaratne, & Camburn (1976) *Continued*									–Worse on school at-tendance and fathers' rat-ings of home behavior –C group also im-proved on 5 measures, worse on 5 –Across all measures: 64% E im-proved vs. 46% C; 8% E worse

	Some Limitations		Treatment	Not Random		Observation			
Walter & Gilmore (1973)	Differential effects of various components of treatment package cannot be ascertained (but further research planned on this); cases not randomly assigned; small N; no follow-up	–Male –5–14 –Referred for "severe out-of-control behavior"	–Training of parents in behavior management of child, individually and in parent groups; –4 wks. –"At least 2" experienced therapists	N = 12	N = 6 attention/ placebo wait list	–Observation of family interaction in home	Yes (independent raters)	No	–E group 61% decrease in targeted behaviors vs. 37% increase C group

Abbreviations used:

C: control or contrast group of cases; the group that does *not* receive the experimental treatment
E: experimental group of cases that *does* receive the experimental treatment
Exp'l: experimental
IP: "Identified Patient"; in these studies, the acting-out adolescent
N: number of cases (in experimental, control, or contrast groups)

(continued)

Table 4-1. Studies of Behavioral Family Intervention* (Continued)

Author	Research Adequacy	Sex-Age-Referral	Methodology	Exp'l N	Control/ Comparison	Measures	Data Un-biased?	Follow-up	Outcome Findings
	Some Limitations			Not Random					
Weathers & Liberman (1975)	As between-group design, defectors inadequate control (but as series of N = 1 designs, multiple baseline is adequate substitute); only curfew monitoring unbiased; no control nonspecific treatment effects	—Male & female —14–17 —Referred by probation dept. as recidivists	—Contingency contracting, communication skills training, videotape feedback —3 sessions training in home; with telephone contacts, total time 5.6 hours per family —Therapist M.A. psychologist	N = 6	N = 16 treatment defectors (also considered as 6 N = 1 studies, with within-subject, multiple-baseline design)	—School attendance and grades —Parent and self-reports re IP behavior —Curfew compliance	? (unknown if school aware of participation in program) No Yes (checked by telephone contact)	3 mo	—No differences between E & C groups, or within E group from baseline, on any measure except some temporary decrease in E group verbal abusiveness

	–Probation violations	Yes (?); not clear if probation dept. aware of participation in program

Abbreviations used:

C: control or contrast group of cases; the group that does *not* receive the experimental treatment

E: experimental group of cases that *does* receive the experimental treatment

Exp'l: experimental

IP: "Identified Patient"; in these studies, the acting-out adolescent

N: number of cases (in experimental, control, or contrast groups)

(continued)

79

Table 4-1. Studies of Behavioral Family Intervention* (Continued)

Author	Research Adequacy	Sex-Age-Referral	Methodology	Exp'l N	Control/Comparison	Measures	Data Un-biased?	Follow-up	Outcome Findings
	Some Limitations			*Matching*					
Wiltz & Patterson (1974)	Ns are small; no control nonspecific treatment effects; no information on therapists or possible confounding effects of multiple therapists	–Male –6–14 –Referred for aggressive behavior	–Contingency-management skills training for parents –12 to 30 hours, 6 weeks to 6 months –"Up to 4 therapists" in parent training groups; no data on therapist characteristics	N = 6	N = 6 wait list	–Observation family interaction in home –Parental self-report	Yes (independent raters) No	No 1 yr	–E significantly improved on targeted IP behaviors, but no generalization (as hypothesized) to non-targeted behaviors

80

| Alvord (1971) | *Inconclusive*
No baseline; no control/contrast group; data not unbiased; follow-up inadequate; no control non-specific treatment effects; no information on attrition; no objective outcome measures | –Male & female
–Age not given, but at least some cases over 14
–Referred as "incorrigible" | –Parent training in home token economy
–Two 1-hour sessions
–Unclear if author was therapist (Ph.D. psychologist) | 26 (plus 2 dropouts) | None | –Parent report of IP behavior

–Parent satisfaction with treatment | No

No | 2 wk | –22 improved according to parent reports; 4 considered failures |

*Abbreviations used:
C: control or contrast group of cases; the group that does *not* receive the experimental treatment
E: experimental group of cases that *does* receive the experimental treatment
Expl: experimental
IP: "Identified Patient"; in these studies, the acting-out adolescent
N: number of cases (in experimental, control, or contrast groups)

(continued)

Table 4-1. Studies of Behavioral Family Intervention* (Continued)

Author	Research Adequacy	Sex-Age-Referral	Methodology	Exp'l N	Control/Comparison	Measures	Data Un-biased?	Follow-up	Outcome Findings
	Inconclusive			Not Random					
Douds, Engelsgjerd, & Collingwood (1977)	No baseline; control group not specified, no evidence of equivalence with E group; no control nonspecific treatment effects; no information on therapists; failures not explored	–Presumably male & female –Presumably adolescents (referred to as "youths") –Youth services program in police dept.; all had committed offenses, 41% were recidivists	–Behavior contracting parents and IP –Parents and youths in separate groups; 15 hours –No information on therapists	1,200 (plus 800 drop-outs; 40% attrition)	Control group referred to but not specified (possibly program defectors?)	–Rearrests –Parent reports of IP behavior	Yes No	"Monthly follow-up" but duration not given	–10.7% rearrests E group vs. 42.7% for "control" group –74% E group improved according to parent reports; no comparative data re "control" group

	Inconclusive							
Tharp & Wetzel (1969)	No control/comparison group; no baselines; data not unbiased; follow-up variable, not all cases followed; no information on high attrition rate; some cases termed failures but no data; no control nonspecific treatment effects; no systematic exploration failures; poor reporting of findings	–Male & female –6–16 –Referred as predelinquents and delinquents	–Instructing "mediators" (parents, teachers) in contingency management of IP home or school behavior	N = 77 (plus 64 dropouts; 45.4% attrition)	None	–Arrests and court records — Yes –Parent reports IP home behavior — No –Teacher reports IP school behavior — No –School grades — ? –Therapists' prognoses — No	"Up to 18 mo"	–Reported improvement most E cases, but reporting by aggregated behavior categories, not cases, and lack of clarity in reporting style render findings impossible to assess

of antisocial behavior of young children may not be generalizable to antisocial behavior problems of adolescents. (Although several investigators [e.g., Levitt, 1957; Robins, 1966, Robins et al., 1975] who studied the outcome of child guidance clinic cases many years later have found that antisocial behavior in preadolescent children, with or without treatment, tends to persist not only into adolescence but also well into adulthood, this speaks to the relative seriousness of this symptomatology in younger children—in contrast to more "neurotic" complaints—not to the effectiveness or ineffectiveness of treatment targeted at antisocial behavior in a person of whatever age.) In most of the studies reported here, the researchers did not report results differentially according to the ages of the children involved. We have, however, included all studies in which at least some adolescents were part of the total sample.

FAMILY TREATMENT OF DELINQUENCY FROM A BEHAVIORAL PERSPECTIVE

Social learning theory and behavior modification techniques have been applied to the problem of juvenile delinquency for approximately the past 20 years. Previous reviews of outcome research concerning this type of treatment with delinquents (Davidson & Seidman, 1974; Lane & Burchard, 1983; Little & Kendall, 1979; Stumphauser, 1970; Zimberoff, 1968) have concluded that preliminary findings were promising, but "methodological weaknesses limit the confidence that can be placed in reported successes" (Davidson & Seidman, p. 998). The following reviews of behavioral interventions that included the family indicate that, with a few outstanding exceptions, the caution still applies that weaknesses of the research limit the confidence that can be placed in reported successes.

The treatments tested in the family behavioral studies

appear to sort themselves out on a continuum according to the active or passive nature of the role assigned to the youngster, which is another way of saying the degree to which *interactional* processes between parent and child were addressed. At one end of this continuum are, first, those projects that focused on training parents in behaviorally based child management techniques, with the child assigned a passive role. Next come treatment efforts that were oriented more to the process of interaction between youngster and parents by an emphasis on specific contracts for behavior change on the part of both parents and child. In this approach, the nature of the contract requires the parents to make changes in some of their behavior as well as requiring behavioral change from the child. Finally, at the far end of the continuum are treatment programs that focus on teaching positive communication and negotiation skills to the family; these may or may not include application of such skills to specific real conflicts.

Behavior management training with families of delinquents centers on development of the parents' ability to use social reinforcers to change the child's behavior. Specific skills taught include (a) targeting aversive behaviors of the child, (b) establishing baseline data, (c) identifying antecedents and reinforcing contingencies, and (d) establishing contingency contracts. In effect, the parents are trained as behavioral therapists for their own child, under the tutelage and supervision of the professional.

For the past 15 years, the Oregon Research Institute (Patterson, 1974; Patterson & Brodsky, 1966; Patterson, Cobb, & Ray, 1973; Patterson, McNeal, Hawkins, & Phelps, 1967; Patterson, Ray, & Shaw, 1968; Patterson & Reid, 1973; Reid & Hendricks, 1973; Walter & Gilmore, 1973; Wiltz & Patterson, 1974) has been developing and evaluating a program to help parents reduce aggressive behavior of their children. Two major assumptions of social learning theory constitute the theoretical framework of the program: that the natural environment of the child is the locus of his learning of behavior and that the behavior must be supported by reinforcers in this environment in order to persist. The program therefore seeks to modify the children's behavior by training parents in the fundamentals of social learning theory and behavioral management techniques.

The age range of the children treated at the Oregon Institute is somewhat younger than that of other studies of delinquency intervention reported here, but at least some of the youngsters were in their teen years. For this reason and also because the work of the Oregon group has implications for prevention of delinquency, we are including in this review those studies of Patterson and his associates that appeared to involve at least some older children.

The intervention program of these researchers consists of didactic education of parents in specific behavior modification techniques, including positive reinforcement and "time out," followed by monitoring (in parents' groups) of the capacity of individual parents to translate the didactic learning into a home child-management program.

A variety of research designs has been used to test the program, ranging from studies of single cases in the early years of its development (Patterson & Brodsky, 1966; Patterson et al., 1967) to a study of five cases (Patterson et al., 1968) to studies with somewhat larger numbers—12 cases (Walter & Gilmore, 1973; Wiltz & Patterson, 1974)—and the most extensive study, which involved 27 families (Patterson, 1974).

In the two studies that included a comparison group of untreated families (Wiltz & Patterson, 1974; Walter and Gilmore, 1973), within only 5 weeks the experimental group of 12 cases in each study demonstrated significant decreases (from 61 to 75 percent) in child aggressive behavior as compared to no significant decrease in the comparison groups (which were waiting-list families in the first study and an attention/placebo group in the second). Reid and Hendricks (1973) of the Oregon Institute compared treatment outcome of 14 boys whose behavior included stealing with that of 11 youngsters who displayed deviant behavior other than stealing. Treatment was found to be twice as effective for the nonstealing group than for children who engaged in this particular deviant behavior. In the 1973 study by Patterson et al. of 13 cases, the targeted behaviors had decreased 47 percent at a 1-year follow-up, although there was no generalization (as was hypothesized would occur) to other nontargeted behaviors of the child; i.e., the parents were unable to transfer their learning about behavioral principles from the specific troublesome child behavior for which they had sought help to other child behavior difficulties.

In Patterson's 1974 study the size of the sample more nearly reached an acceptable number for group-comparison research (N = 27). In this study a true control group was not utilized since the experimental families were matched with "normal" families who did *not* have a problem child. In contrast, however, to the early research of Minuchin, Montalvo, Guerney, Rosman, and Schumer (1967), which was flawed by their attempt to utilize such a nonproblematic group as a "control," the Oregon Institute's rationale was more acceptable in that they utilized the rates of "normal" aggression in the nonproblematic families as the norm toward which it was hoped the families with aggressive children could move as a result of treatment. In other words, a "normal" amount of aggressive behavior was hypothesized to exist for well-functioning children, and this quantitative measure was utilized as the principal criterion of effectiveness for the treated group. The findings demonstrated that the aggressive behavior of the experimental cases had decreased after treatment, by an average of 60 percent, to the normal range of the comparison families and remained at that level at the 1-year follow-up. This reduction was accompanied by salient changes in parent-child relationships, including significant increases in positive exchanges and decreases in the use of punishment.

Taken individually, each of these studies does not represent conclusive evidence of the effectiveness of the intervention in modifying the aggressive behaviors of children, since each has some methodological flaws. The small numbers of the first several studies have already been noted. The sample size of the study by Patterson in 1974 is more nearly adequate, but random assignment would have been a better way than matching to achieve equivalence of groups. The positive findings of this group of studies, in addition to the earlier studies by these researchers, does, however, represent an accumulation of evidence that cannot be lightly dismissed as a conclusion of the effectiveness of the program.

The failure of the training to generalize to other behaviors of the child, however, would seem to indicate that parental child-management training is not sufficient for most cases. Because the children ranged in age from six to fourteen years and no breakdown is given on outcome in terms of the age of the child involved, it is not possible to determine if development of parental child-management skills *alone* is sufficient to bring about behavioral change in an acting-out adolescent. It may further be speculated that the younger child is more under the physical and psychological control of the parents than the adolescent, who is at a life stage characterized by a need for more independence from parents. Parental training techniques may therefore be more appropriate for behavioral problems of preadolescent children than for adolescent delinquents. But this is at present not known and therefore needs to be researched.

A strength of the research component of the Oregon Institute program is its insistence on periodic reports by parents after the conclusion of treatment. In view of this highly commendable but rare effort by any treatment or research program to continue to gather data on the duration of the effects of the intervention, it is unfortunate that these authors fail to relate a reduction in the children's aggressive behaviors as reported by parents to more objective measures such as reports of school behavior and police and court contacts. Yet the reported success rates are sufficiently impressive that it is to be hoped that further research by the Oregon group will continue to be conducted and published.

Behavior contracting as an intervention with families of delinquents is described as "a means of scheduling the exchange of positive reinforcements between two or more persons" (Stuart, 1971). According to Stuart, effective contracts contain five elements: (a) details of privileges that each party expects to gain after fulfilling his/her responsibilities, (b) details of the responsibilities essential to securing each privilege, (c) a system of sanctions for failure to meet responsibilities, (d) a clause that assures positive reinforcement for compliance with the terms of the contract, and (e) a method of keeping track of the rate of positive reinforcement given and received.

Several studies were located in which a contracting process concerning mutual behaviors of parents and child was a major feature. The publications of Stuart and Lott (1972); Stuart and Tripodi (1973); Jayaratne, Stuart, and Tripodi (1974); Stuart, Jayaratne, and Tripodi (1976); and Stuart, Tripodi, Jayaratne, and Camburn (1976) describe a 4-year "Family and School Consultation Project" that utilized as the primary intervention behavioral contracting between adolescents and their parents and teachers. The project focused on predelinquent and delinquent boys and girls ranging in age from twelve to over fifteen years. The 1972–1973 study also sought to examine the relative impact of various time lengths of treatment: experimental families were randomly assigned to 15 days, 45 days, or 90 days of treatment (corresponding to 6, 18, and 36 hours of professional contact). The first phase of the project, reported in this study, had not been in existence long enough for sufficient court record data to be available as an outcome measure.

No major differences were found according to the length of treatment, and outcome seemed to be a function of characteristics of the particular therapist as much as, or more than, characteristics of the clients. Other findings from this study concerning the overall effectiveness of behavior contracting with adolescent delinquents are difficult to assess. The experimental groups did appear to improve somewhat over the control group composed of families who had refused treatment, but findings were mixed.

In 1976 Stuart, Jayaratne, and Tripodi reported on a study of 30 cases; and Stuart, Tripodi, Jayaratne, and Camburn reported on one involving 57 families. Control/ comparison group composition was better in these projects than in the 1972–1973 research, in which families who refused treatment constituted the control group (service refusers are obviously different in at least one important respect from families who accept treatment). In the 1976 studies an activity-group placebo condition represented the contrast group in the first project, and families who were refused treatment by the project staff were the control group for the second study. (However, in the first study half of the "placebo only" subjects also received from school personnel some components of the treatment package, thus compromising their value as a true contrast to the experimental treatment; and in the second study some of the control families who were refused treatment by the project sought alternative help elsewhere in the community.) Both studies demonstrated only mild improvement of the experimental group, and this on "soft" measures such as teachers' and parents' evaluations of the adolescent's behavior; "harder" indicators such as school attendance and grades demonstrated deterioration. The authors conclude that these results of their research "clearly indicate that the single technique of behavioral contracting is no panacea" (Stuart, Tripodi, Jayaratne, and Camburn, 1976, p. 260). The authors further speculate that the finding of a deterioration in the father-adolescent relationship might reflect an unanticipated impact of the behavioral technique on the systemic power structure of the family organization. At least some behaviorists therefore seem to be moving away from a monocular belief in the power of behavioral technology alone to a recognition that systemic variables of family dynamics also may be playing a salient role in the problem situation (and may call for other than behavioral interventions).

The 1969 project of Tharp and Wetzel also can be classified as a treatment effort that highlighted behavioral contracting, although treatment varied a good deal from case to case and therapist to therapist, as well as in the amount of professional time invested in different cases. The research portion of this project seems to have been added in a post-hoc manner, with the result that although the authors claim outstanding success for their intervention approach, the limitations of the research design, execution, and reporting are such that the study provides "inconclusive evidence" for the efficacy of this intervention.

Douds, Engelsgjerd, and Collingwood (1977) applied behavioral contracting as the major intervention in a police department youth services program with a very large number of adolescent delinquents (N = 1,200). Rearrests were reported to be substantially less for the experimental group than for a "control" group (which unfortunately is not further described). The time period over which recidivism data were gathered is also not clarified.

Alvord (1971) utilized behavior contracting in the form of a home token economy system. The age range of the children involved is not given, but apparently at least some of the youngsters were older than fourteen, as the author describes his 4 failure cases out of the total sample of 26 as older adolescents who were beyond the physical and psychological control of the parents and therefore unimpressed by the token economy instituted by the parents. The research design and implementation of this study render its findings "inconclusive evidence."

Part of what seems to happen in successful behavioral contracting is that a *system* of parent-child *interactions* is being changed, not merely behaviors. The findings of the 1976 study of Stuart, Tripodi, Jayaratne, and Camburn indicate that an iatrogenic correlation may exist between behavioral intervention and negative impact on the family structure and interactions unless the therapists have a sophisticated awareness of the possibility of this consequence and take steps to prevent it.

Further clinical experience and research are certainly needed to test the viability of behavioral contracting, probably as but one component of a treatment package. It may be hypothesized that contracting will be most effective for those cases in which parental approval is still very important to the adolescent, where he/she is not substantially involved in a prodelinquent peer culture outside the home, and where parental attitudes toward the youngster are not so rejecting that they will not permit contracting to change their characteristic ways of relating to the adolescent.

Negotiation/communication skills training involves efforts to increase positive verbal exchanges and decrease verbal criticism among family members. Small group studies have indicated that "defensive" communication—verbal and nonverbal behaviors that are threatening or punishing to others and reciprocally provoke defensive behaviors from others—is characteristic of nonproductive systems demonstrating self-defeating programs (Gibb, 1961; Jacob, 1975). Alexander and Parsons (1973) utilized the concept of "defensive-supportive communication" in evaluating the interactive behavior of normal and delinquent families. In this approach, training in communication skills is often combined with training in conflict negotiation: the family is taught to identify the issues involved in conflict situations and how to negotiate an acceptable (and usually compromise) solution.

The studies by Alexander and his associates (Alexander, Barton, Schiavo, & Parsons, 1976; Alexander & Parsons, 1973; Klein, Alexander, & Parsons, 1977; Parsons & Alexander, 1973) are outstanding in a number of respects. Despite some methodological shortcomings, they are probably the best of the total group of behavioral studies in terms of research design and execution. Further, the experimental treatment involved represents an attempt to move beyond an overly narrow "behavior only" perspective to take into consideration and attempt to change as well some of the systemic structure and process of the family, or at least of the parent(s)-child family subgroup. The other behavioral treatments reported here may well have inadvertently brought about some systemic change (for better or for worse), but the projects undertaken by Alexander and his co-workers were the first to utilize family system theory as well as social learning theory as a conceptual base.

The cases reported represented nearly equal proportions of boys and girls, aged from 13 to 16 years, who were referred by the juvenile court for status offenses such as running away and truancy and for law violations such as shoplifting and use of alcohol or drugs. No information is given concerning such other variables as family composition, socioeconomic status, and history of previous delinquency.

The Institute staff first attempted to identify specific family communication patterns that have some empirical support as distinguishing delinquent families. According to previous research (Duncan, 1968; Mischler & Waxler, 1968; Stuart, 1968; Winter & Ferreira, 1969), delinquent families are more silent and less egalitarian, and they have fewer positive communications than families without a delinquent child.

In the Parsons and Alexander 1973 study, 40 families were randomly assigned to one of four groups: two experimental groups, one of which received both pre- and post-testing and the other post-testing only; a post-test only attention/placebo group; or a pre- and post-test no-treatment control group. The families were videotaped resolving a "problem situation" before and after treatment. Observers were trained to assess the families' interactions in terms of equality of speech, silence, and frequency and duration of positive interruptions.

In the Alexander and Parsons study of 1973, 46 families received the experimental treatment of communication skills training plus behavioral contracting, with the goal of changing not only the targeted behaviors of the child but also the way in which family members related to one another. Two comparison groups received from other community agencies either client-centered group therapy or "eclectic" (apparently mostly psychodynamically and insight-oriented) family therapies. A waiting list represented the control group. Measures of family conflict resolution skills, rated by independent judges, demonstrated a significant superiority of the experimental treatment over the alternative treatments as well as over no treatment.

It is of note that the psychodynamic family therapy modality had much the poorest success rate, both in altering family interaction and in reduction of delinquent behavior—poorer even than the no-treatment control group (73 percent recidivism versus 50 percent for the control group).

In another publication reporting on this same study, Klein et al. (1977) examined the impact of the experimental treatment 2½ to 3½ years later on the *siblings* of the original delinquents and found that subsequent delinquency of these younger children was substantially less in those families that had received the experimental treatment.

A smaller study (Parsons and Alexander, 1973) demonstrated the superiority of the experimental intervention over an attention/placebo condition.

In 1976 Alexander et al. reported on an examination of characteristics of the therapist as they related to case outcome. They found that relationship skills of the therapist, as well as what they call "structuring" skills (the therapist's ability to maintain focus in the treatment contact), were both important and were correlated with positive outcome.

This Western States Institute group carried out some of the best research designs in the group of studies assessed. However, the methodology is not without some weaknesses. Although the researchers are to be credited with including dropouts in their analysis of recidivism rates, attrition constituted 24 percent of the total sample, and these dropouts were not analyzed to determine in what ways they differed from the experimental and control groups. This, plus the sizable proportion of cases who refused involvement in the program, places a limitation on the generalizability of the findings concerning the treatment approach. The research also would have been strengthened if the total sample size in the Alexander and Parsons study of 1973, and the size of each group, had been larger—particularly the no-treatment group whose size is disproportionately smaller than that of the experimental and contrast conditions. Another weakness is the failure to utilize a consistent follow-up period: recidivism was studied for the four treatment groups at a 6- to 18-month interval following completion of treatment. However, it might be argued that youngsters who were followed up only 6 months after treatment had not had as much time to engage in further delinquent behavior. The researchers might have presented better evidence to counteract this alternative explanation if they had followed up all cases after a similar time period or at least had included a breakdown of recidivism rates according to the various follow-up periods employed.

Finally, since examination of the recorded recidivism of the Identified Patients' siblings was conducted from 2½ to 3½ years later, it is puzzling why the researchers, while they were perusing court and other records, did not check the recidivism of the original delinquents at the same time.

The findings of the studies by Alexander and his associates are relevant to the issue with which we are concerned: delinquency prevention/rehabilitation and involvement of the family in the rehabilitation process. The researchers present detailed information about patterns of family communication that have been demonstrated to be associated with delinquent behavior by the child. The findings supply reasonably valid evidence that their program was effective in reducing delinquent behaviors of a group of status offenders for 6 to 18 months following completion of the program. Famiglietti (1981), in his review of this study concludes that although the findings of Alexander and his associates are useful, further research is needed to "examine other aspects of family life that have been associated with delinquency, such as the nature of the parents' discipline and supervision" (p. 67).

A number of other researchers have tested the treatment approach of Alexander and his associates. Robin et al. (1977) and Robin (1979, 1981, 1983) reported on two studies utilizing "PSCT": problem-solving communication training. Although this intervention was demonstrated to be superior to a wait-list control in the first study and to both a control group and a comparison with nonbehavioral family therapy in the 1981 study, results were not otherwise clear cut. In the 1977 work, for example, although experimental families improved significantly on communication skills as audiotaped in the office setting, there was no generalization to home behavior. In the 1981 study, client self-reports did indicate that changes were maintained at home, at least over a brief follow-up period of 8 to 10 weeks. Kifer et al. (1974) also reported improvement of families receiving training in communication and negotiation skills in a small (N = 3) single-subject design study. Patterson et al. in 1973 found improvement in targeted behaviors for 11 of 13 families receiving a combination of communication/negotiation skills training plus training of the parents in behavior management principles, but again, no generalization to nontargeted behaviors.

Shostak (1977) compared the outcome of "family-oriented behavior therapy," in the Alexander and co-workers model with 8 adolescents and their families to individual behavior therapy for the youngster alone and a wait-list control. Findings were somewhat mixed but were generally better for the family treatment, and recidivism rates were decidedly lower for the experimental intervention. Individual behavior therapy fared no better than no treatment in terms of general results and had the *highest* recidivism rate (88 percent to 75 percent for the no-treatment control group and 25 percent for the family-oriented experimental treatment).

Weathers and Liberman (1975) also combined communication skills training with other techniques, in this case contingency contracting and videotape feedback to the family of their own interaction. Perhaps because of the brevity of the intervention (only three in-home training sessions), the treatment failed to show any important impact. Klees (1979) also failed to find evidence of substantial change in his small (N = 5) single-subject design study, possibly because of the fact that this researcher seemed to be dealing with much more disadvantaged families, with delinquency of a more hard-core type than in the other studies (families were so difficult to motivate that although they were paid $100 for attending all 10 sessions of the treatment program, almost half dropped out).

Table 4-2.   Studies of Nonbehavioral Family Intervention*

Author	Research Adequacy	Sex-Age-Referral	Methodology	Exp'l N	Control/Comparison	Measures	Data Unbiased?	Follow-up	Outcome Findings
	High Credibility				Random				
Byles & Maurice (1979)	But not enough information given to assess objectivity of outcome measures; nonspecific effects of treatment and impact further treatment some cases not addressed	Male & female –6–14 (so some adolescents) –At least one police contact; living at home	–Crisis family therapy –9 social worker and RN therapists from outpatient psychiatry clinic; received supervision –"Short-term" ($\overline{X}$6, but range 1–7+); however, some referred for continued treatment elsewhere	N = 70 (+65 refused service +19 "missed cases")	N = 151 received "traditional" Police Youth Bureau services	–Recidivism: number and seriousness police and court charges	? (Did police know which adolescents in E or C group?)	24 mo after entry into project	"No effect". –Higher E recidivism, also higher for E siblings than C siblings, except for E cases with 2 previous offenses (57% recidivism E vs. 92% C). –C significantly higher recidivism in E families who accepted

98

							expl'l treatment (69%) vs. refusers (57%).
	High Credibility						
Ferreira & Winter (1966)	Research not designed as study of outcome per se so selection of E & C groups not inappropriate; control nonspecific factors, follow-up, and use of multiple indicators not relevant to study	Larger sample of 40 disturbed families contained 6 delinquents age 13–20 and 2 "acting-out" adolescents, age 14; all male.	—Conjoint family therapy, not further described. —Therapists not described other than as trainees —Tested after 6 mo of therapy	N = 10 *Random* N = 13 "Normal" families (no treatment)	Family interaction: "spontaneous agreement," "decision-time," "choice-fulfillment" (choices of individuals adopted by family)	Yes (independent rater)	None —No change either group on family interaction measures

(continued)

Abbreviations used:

C: control or contrast group of cases; the group that does *not* receive the experimental treatment

E: experimental group of cases that *does* receive the experimental treatment

Expl: experimental

IP: "Identified Patient"; in these studies, the acting-out adolescent

N: number of cases (in experimental, control, or contrast groups)

Table 4-2. Studies of Nonbehavioral Family Intervention* (Continued)

Author	Research Adequacy	Sex-Age-Referral	Methodology	Exp'l N	Control/Comparison	Measures	Data Unbiased?	Follow-up	Outcome Findings
	High Credibility			*Random*					
(1968)	focus; possible effect pretest on post-test belied by findings, but no information re what "family therapy" consisted of	Same	Same	N = 10	N = 10	Family interaction; "information" exchanged by members, amount of time in "silence" (audiotaped)	Same	Same	–No significant change in either group
						(audiotaped)			
	High Credibility			*Non-Random*					
Haley (1964)	Research not designed as study of outcome per se, so selection of	Larger sample of 40 disturbed families contained	–Family therapy, not further described	N = 6	N = 6 "Normal" families (no treatment)	Family interaction (communication sequences)	Yes (independent rater)	None	–E: Average change 3.15% on family inter-

100

E & C groups not inappropriate; control nonspecific factors, and use of multiple indicators not relevant to study focus; possible effect pre-test on post-test belied by findings, but no information re what "family therapy" consisted of; no control nonspecific effects	6 delinquents age 13–20, 2 "acting-out" adolescents, age 14; all male	–Therapists 4 trainees, 2 experienced therapists –Tested after 6 mo therapy	action measures –C: Average change 2.36% –Samples too small to establish statistical significance

(continued)

*Abbreviations used:
C: control or contrast group of cases; the group that does *not* receive the experimental treatment
E: experimental group of cases that *does* receive the experimental treatment
Exp'l: experimental
IP: "Identified Patient"; in these studies, the acting-out adolescent
N: number of cases (in experimental, control, or contrast groups)

Table 4-2. Studies of Nonbehavioral Family Intervention* (Continued)

Author	Research Adequacy	Sex-Age-Referral	Methodology	Exp'l N	Control Comparison	Measures	Data Unbiased?	Follow-up	Outcome Findings
	Some Limitations			*Not Random*					
Evans, Chagoya, & Rakoff (1971)	Study was not focused on outcome per se but outcome findings confounded by therapists' biased selection of E & C groups; intervention multiple so effects any one component cannot be discerned; outcome data not unbiased; follow-up at variable time periods, and data on only 44%;	–Male & female –12–21, $\overline{X}$ = 16 –Referred to psychiatric ward; some "character disorder," acting-out delinquent	–Obligatory policy that all adolescent patients receive "conjoint family therapy" during and post hospitalization –Study examined why some patients did not receive family therapy, and outcomes different treatments –Some of both E & C groups also received individ-	N = 50. Therapist chose family therapy	N = 50. Therapist chose alternate treatment	–Therapists' clinical impressions at termination –Parent responses to follow-up letter	No No	Variable time postdischarge: from few days to 2 yr	–"Obvious improvement" symptom removal and return to work/school: E 64% vs. 46% C group –"Slight improvement": E 28% vs. 10% C group –"No improvement E 8% vs. 44% C group

failures not explored	ual therapy and/or medication, ECT		−44% response 66% agreed with hospital assessment outcome; 16% reported less improved, 18% more improved
	−Therapists 23 psychiatric residents, "novices in family therapy"		
	−Hospital stay 3 days–5 mo $\overline{X}$ = 3 mo; post-hospital treatment 9 days–36 mo, $\overline{X}$ = 3 mo		−Family therapy cases were initially healthier, higher socioeconomic status

(*continued*)

Table 4-2. Studies of Nonbehavioral Family Intervention* (Continued)

Author	Research Adequacy	Sex-Age-Referral	Methodology	Exp'l N	Control/Comparison	Measures	Data Unbiased?	Follow-up	Outcome Findings
	Some Limitations			*Not Random*					
Garrigan & Bambrick (1975)	E & C groups not randomly assigned; matched only on age & IQ; outcomes measures subjective; no follow-up	−Male −11–15 −Referred to special school for (nonorganic, nonpsychotic) academic and behavioral problems	−Short-term family therapy utilizing Zuk's "go-between" method −5 therapists doctoral students, received training −6 sessions	N = 9	N = 9	−Parents' and IP's perceptions of family adjustment (interaction); IP's perception of parental attitudes; IP's self-concept −Teacher's report of school behavior	No Questionable	1 wk 1 wk	−E superior most measures except IP's self-concept −No differences
	Some Limitations			*Random*					
Garrigan & Bambrick (1977)	Only unbiased measure that of "blind" rater re	−Male & female	−Short-term family therapy utilizing Zuk's	N = 12 + 2 dropout	N = 14 Wait list: after testing, given parent group	−Parents' and IP's reports of family ad-	No	1 wk	−Mixed results: parents perceived im-

104

	"go-between" method	discussion	justment and relationships		provement; IPs did not
classroom behaviors; no follow-up					
-11-17	-5 therapists; assume doctoral students as in 1975 study		-Anxiety of family members	No	
-Referred to special school for (nonorganic, nonpsychotic) academic and behavioral problems	-10 sessions in 16 wk		-Parents' estimates IP's symptoms	No	
			-Devereaux scale re IP's classroom behavior	Yes: rater teacher "blind" re whether child in E or C group	-Improved classroom behavior in E group
				?	
			-Return to regular school	No	-5 E group IPs returned vs 1 C group

(continued)

Abbreviations used:

C: control or contrast group of cases; the group that does *not* receive the experimental treatment
E: experimental group of cases that *does* receive the experimental treatment
Exp'l: experimental
IP: "Identified Patient"; in these studies, the acting-out adolescent
N: number of cases (in experimental, control, or contrast groups)

Table 4-2. Studies of Nonbehavioral Family Intervention* (Continued)

Author	Research Adequacy	Sex-Age-Referral	Methodology	Exp'l N	Control/Comparison	Measures	Data Unbiased?	Follow-up	Outcome Findings
				Random					
Ginsberg (1977)	*Some Limitations* Unclear if audiotaped measures were unbiased; other measures not unbiased; no control nonspecific effects; no follow-up	–Male $\overline{X}$ of E = 12.6; C = 13.2 (so some older than 13) –Subjects were volunteers for re-	"Relationship enhancement" program for fathers and sons Therapist author (Ph.D. candidate, psychology) Sessions: 10 wk for 2 hours in	N = 14 plus 4 dropout	N = 15 plus 4 dropout	–Communication skills (audiotaped) –Unobtrusive observation communication skills (audiotaped)	–? (unclear if independent rater used)	None	–E significant improvement over pre-test and C group on observed communication skills, general communication

106

						–No difference self-concept
					None	
			–Self-report re general communication –No			
			–Self-report re general relationship –No			
			–Self-concept –No			Same findings; all changes occurred during treatment, not during wait
			Same	Same		
search project; not selected on basis presence or absence of problems	group	15 control cases later received exp'l treatment	None			

(continued)

Abbreviations used:

C: control or contrast group of cases; the group that does *not* receive the experimental treatment
E: experimental group of cases that *does* receive the experimental treatment
Exp'l: experimental
IP: "Identified Patient"; in these studies, the acting-out adolescent
N: number of cases (in experimental, control, or contrast groups)

Table 4-2. Studies of Nonbehavioral Family Intervention* (Continued)

Author	Research Adequacy	Sex-Age-Referral	Methodology	Exp'l N	Control/ Comparison	Measures	Data Un-biased?	Follow-up	Outcome Findings
	Some Limitations			*Not Random*					
Gluck, Tanner, Sullivan, & Erickson (1964)	–But no control/ contrast groups; follow-up too brief, data not unbiased.	–Male & female –13–17 –Study reports follow-up evaluation of first 55 cases seen in new child guidance	–Varied service: from brief evaluative contacts with parents to "long-term intensive psychotherapy" with child and parents, apparently no conjoint therapy of parents plus child	N = 12	None	Mail report from parents re status child's symptoms; phone contact if no immediate response (response from 54 of original sample of 55 cases)	No	6 mo	–In adolescent subgroup, 69.4% of symptoms improved –No significant relation between child's being seen and

108

			symptom abatement (total sample)
			–But "striking and significant relation between report of improvement and contact of both parents plus child"

| | clinic; age range 3–17. This review focuses on those 12 cases with IP aged 13–17; presumably at least some of these were "acting-out," "rebellious," "pre-delinquent" or "delinquent" behavior | –2 therapists "experienced in child guidance"

 –"Most of families seen for relatively few . . . contacts" | |

Abbreviations used:

C: control or contrast group of cases; the group that does *not* receive the experimental treatment
E: experimental group of cases that *does* receive the experimental treatment
Expl: experimental
IP: "Identified Patient"; in these studies, the acting-out adolescent
N: number of cases (in experimental, control, or contrast groups)

(continued)

Table 4-2. Studies of Nonbehavioral Family Intervention* (Continued)

Author	Research Adequacy	Sex-Age-Referral	Methodology	Exp'l N	Control/ Comparison	Measures	Data Un-biased?	Follow-up	Outcome Findings
Maskin & Brookins (1974)	*Some Limitations* Study not focused on outcome per se, but meaningfulness of outcome data would have been enhanced by control or contrast group, or at least comparison with court statistics on recidivism in state population of adolescent delinquents	–Female –13–17 –Referred to juvenile hall as first offenders; sample all girls admitted over 1 yr	–Parent and child counseling during 4 mo aftercare –Therapists: no information –6 mo residential treatment plus 4 mo aftercare	E groups matched: E #1: 30 single parent E #2: 56 both parents E # 3: 40 foster parents	None	Recidivism: 2 or more detentions during 10 mo program or institutionalization after program completion	Yes	None No information on length of follow-up	–Recidivism significantly higher in group living with both natural parents: 68% vs. 23% single parent, & 53% in foster home

Maskin (1976)	*Some Limitations* No information on follow-up time re institutionalization; no information on therapists either program; no information on what aftercare consisted of in each program; no control non-specific treatment effects	−Male −15–17 −First-time offenders in residential corrections programs	−E group emphasis "parent-child interaction through individual and group counseling" −Therapists: no information −6 mo residential treatment plus 4 mo aftercare	N = 30	*Matching* N = 30 ranch work-oriented program 6 mo; 4 mo aftercare	Recidivism: 2 or more detentions during 10 mo of program or institutionalization after program completion	Yes	Yes	None	No information on length of follow-up	−Significantly less recidivism E group (17%) than C group (77%)

(continued)

Table 4-2. Studies of Nonbehavioral Family Intervention* (Continued)

Author	Research Adequacy	Sex-Age-Referral	Methodology	Expl N	Control/ Comparison	Measures	Data Un-biased?	Follow-up	Outcome Findings
Postner, Guttman, Sigal, Epstein, & Rakoff (1971)	*Some Limitations* For study of outcome (in contrast to process study of 1967) control/ contrast group needed; cases selected; outcome data not unbiased; no control nonspecific effects treatment	–Male, & female –boys $\overline{X}$ = 11.5, girls $\overline{X}$ = 15.5 –Referred for variety children's problems, including behavior	–Conjoint family therapy, focus on communication, feelings, interpretation –Therapists 3 psychiatric residents, 2 social workers, 3 psychologists, 1 psychiatrist; received training –5 to 44 sessions, $\overline{X}$ = 21	N = 11 (From larger sample in Sigal et al. 1967 study, selected as cases in treatment long enough to make audiotapes)	None	–20-min audiotapes of 2nd, 6th, 12th, 18th, & 24th sessions; analyzed for both therapist and family verbal behavior –Follow-up interviews by senior staff (authors?) re progress/outcome	Yes (independent raters) ? (Interview protocols rated by independent raters, but question-	Same	–Overall outcome data given on only 9 cases: 5 (56%) "good outcome"; 4 (44%) "Poor outcome" –Good outcome cases characterized by passive, low involvement mother and verbal father (reverse in poor outcome), increase in

112

	Some Limitations							
Sigal, Rakoff & Epstein (1967)	Study focus was process, not outcome per se, so lack control/contrast group not inappropriate, but cases selected; outcome data not unbiased; apparently some	−Male, female −boys, $\overline{X}$ = 11.5, girls, $\overline{X}$ = 15.5 −Referred for variety children's	−Conjoint family therapy, focus on communication, interpretation feelings, inter- −Therapists 3 psychiatric residents, 2 social workers, 3 psy-	N = 19 Selected	None	−Study compared case progress or outcome to therapist's judgment, while case ongoing, re family's cooperation with	No (able if data totally unbiased)	−Judgment re family cooperation not predictive of later outcome −No cases total improvement; −74% some therapist activity to family generally and decrease output to IP (reverse in poor outcome)

(continued)

*Abbreviations used:

C: control or contrast group of cases; the group that does *not* receive the experimental treatment

E: experimental group of cases that *does* receive the experimental treatment

Exp'l: experimental

IP: "Identified Patient"; in these studies, the acting-out adolescent

N: number of cases (in experimental, control, or contrast groups)

Table 4-2. Studies of Nonbehavioral Family Intervention* (Continued)

Author	Research Adequacy	Sex-Age-Referral	Methodology	Exp'l N	Control/Comparison	Measures	Data Unbiased?	Follow-up	Outcome Findings
Sigal, Rakoff & Epstein (1967) Continued	Some Limitations cases terminated early, but data do not differentiate; no control non-specific effects treatment	problems, including behavior	chologists, 1 psychiatrist; received training −5 to 44 sessions $\overline{X} = 21$	Random		therapist —Interviews of family by "senior staff" (authors?) re progress/outcome	(? Interview protocols rated by independent raters but questionable if data totally unbiased)	14 mo after treatment began (i.e., some, but not all, cases closed)	improvement; −26% no change or worse

114

	Some Limitations				*Random*		
Wellisch, Vincent, & Ro-Trock (1976)	Only one of outcome measures unbiased; 3 mo follow-up too brief for re-hospitalization measure; possible bias against individual therapy by therapists for that group; possible question professional qualifications occupational therapists used for E group; no control nonspecific treatment effects	–Presumably male & female –13–22 –Inpatient psychiatric setting: some patients schizophrenic, others had behavior problems	–Conjoint family therapy, focus on communication, present problems, psychodynamics. –Therapists: 2 male-female teams for family therapy; 2 doctoral candidates in psychology and public health, previous training family therapy; 2 occupational therapists, previous	N = 14 Focus on problem-solving skills re life conflicts, feelings, psychodynamics.	–Self-reports marital communication, parent-child communication, IP's perceptions of self and of parents –Family problem solving (videotaped) –Mother's report of rehospitalization of IP, days to re-	No Yes (independent raters) ?	3 mo	–No change either group marital communication; no significant differences E group on parent-child communication; no change self-perceptions. –Mixed findings problem solving; no clear improvement either group

Abbreviations used:

C: control or contrast group of cases; the group that does *not* receive the experimental treatment
E: experimental group of cases that *does* receive the experimental treatment
Exp'l: experimental
IP: "Identified Patient"; in these studies, the acting-out adolescent
N: number of cases (in experimental, control, or contrast groups)

(continued)

Table 4-2. Studies of Nonbehavioral Family Intervention*

Author	Research Adequacy	Sex-Age-Referral	Methodology	Exp'l N	Control/Comparison	Measures	Data Unbiased?	Follow-up	Outcome Findings
Wellisch, Vincent, & Ro-Trock (1976) Continued			training family therapy; 2 therapists for individual treatment C group appear same as in family therapy teams, previous training psychodynamic individual therapy as well as family therapy -Sessions: 8 each treatment			turn to school/work			-Rehosp: 0% E vs. 43% C -Return to functioning: $\overline{X}$ = 7.5 days E vs. 15.4 days C
Baron & Feeney (1976)	*Inconclusive* Not random assignment to E or C; no follow-up; data on which outcome conclu-	-Male & female -"Youths," (presumably	-Short-term family crisis therapy -Therapists pro-	*Not Random* "601 Project": N = 803 "602 Project":	N = 558 regular probation service ents	Court petitions by parents -Informal	-Unclear whether under control or influence	None	"601 Project" -Court petitions: E 3.7% vs. 19.8% C group

	(...adolescents)	(...bation officers trained in family therapy)	Not given	Not given	(...probations)	(...of therapist)	
...sions based not given; no statistical analysis of significance of differences found; no control nonspecific effects; failures not explored; some data not unbiased; intervention not clearly described	–Court program: "601" project status offenders; "602" project minor to moderately severe offenses	–5 sessions			–Days spent in detention		–Detention: 50% reduction E group
					–Recidivism	–Yes	–Recidivism: E 46.3% vs. 54.2% C group
					–Cost of services	–Yes	–Cost: E less than half of regular service
							"602 Project" Recidivism: E 21.6% vs. 38.1% C group. No statistical analysis

(continued)

Abbreviations used:

C: control or contrast group of cases; the group that does *not* receive the experimental treatment
E: experimental group of cases that *does* receive the experimental treatment
Exp'l: experimental
IP: "Identified Patient"; in these studies, the acting-out adolescent
N: number of cases (in experimental, control, or contrast groups)

Table 4-2. Studies of Nonbehavioral Family Intervention* (Continued)

Author	Research Adequacy	Sex-Age-Referral	Methodology	Exp'l N	Control/Comparison	Measures	Data Unbiased?	Follow-up	Outcome Findings
	Inconclusive			*Not Random*					
Beal & Duckro (1977)	Not random assignment to E or C; E & C groups not equivalent (E families volunteers for program, C group not volunteers, so bias in favor of E group); data highly biased; data tables disagree with text; no follow-up; no control nonspecific effects; no exploration failures; intervention so multiple that effects of any one component cannot be discerned	—Male & female —Age not given, presumably at least some adolescents —Juvenile status offender unit in a court or probation department	—Short-term eclectic family therapy (crisis intervention plus other family techniques and group therapy) —Therapists: unclear if probation officers; received training in family and group counseling —6–8 sessions	N = 44 who accepted offer of family therapy (but outcome data given on N = 46)	N = 54 cases seen in agency the year before family program started (outcome data given on 51)	—Therapist and family judgment re family satisfactory functioning —Referred to mental health agency without court contact —Court petitions —Family satisfaction with program	No No No No	None	—83% (of 46 E cases) terminated ("approx. 30%") or referred ("approx. 50%") vs. 65% C group (statistically significant) —17% (of 46 E cases) court petition vs. 35% C group (statistically significant) —Satisfaction "highly favorable" (no data)

118

Coughlin & Wimberger (1968)								
Inconclusive								

| Exp'l cases arbitrarily selected; no control/comparison group; outcome data biased; intervention so multiple that effects of any one component cannot be discerned; confounding effect of multiple therapists; no control of nonspecific | –Male

–13–17

–Referred for severe parent-child conflict (some delinquent) | –Multiple family group therapy, plus parents' group, children's group, individual family therapy

–Therapists 2 psychiatrists, 2 social workers

–18 sessions | 10 "arbitrarily selected" by therapists from wait list (1 dropout) | None | –Family perception of improvement at termination

–Therapists' clinical impressions at termination | No

No | None | –At termination 8 families reported improvement (but 2 of these requested further therapy, and therapists recommended continued therapy for 3 more, so only 3 families considered by |

(continued)

Abbreviations used:

C: control or contrast group of cases; the group that does *not* receive the experimental treatment
E: experimental group of cases that *does* receive the experimental treatment
Exp'l: experimental
IP: "Identified Patient"; in these studies, the acting-out adolescent
N: number of cases (in experimental, control, or contrast groups)

119

Table 4-2. Studies of Nonbehavioral Family Intervention* (Continued)

Author	Research Adequacy	Sex-Age-Referral	Methodology	Exp'l N	Control/Comparison	Measures	Data Un-biased?	Follow-up	Outcome Findings
Coughlin & Wimberger (1968) *Continued*	treatment effects; authors' claim of success belied by their data (of 10 families, only 1 six mo later reported IP had not left home and family relations satisfactory)					Mail questionnaire to family	No	6 mo	selves and therapists to be functioning so satisfactorily that further help is not needed) —Of 5 responses, 4 families felt helped. In 3, IP had moved out of home (to foster care, military, college)

	Inconclusive						
Cutter & Hallowitz (1962)	Selection process for cases unclear; no control/comparison group; outcome criteria biased; outcome data not finalized and vague; intervention not clearly described and highly variable; follow-up variable in quantity and quality; therapists not described; no control nonspecific treatment effects; no exploration failures; data not unbiased	−Male & female −90% 12–16 −Referred as delinquents, school behavior, home behavior	−"Treatment of family unit" with some individual, dyad, etc., sessions −Sessions: from 2 to several years; variable schedule (weekly to several months apart) −Authors are psychiatrist and social worker; unclear if other therapists involved	N = 56 "currently active" with agency None	−Unclear whose judgment; no objective evidence −Symptom resolution or abatement No −School adjustment No −"Improved family relationships" No	Variable: some but not all families followed by phone or personal contact, some for several months or years	−No cases reported as fully meeting outcome criteria −61% progress felt to be good −25% some progress, but prognosis questionable −14% "no detectable gains whatsoever"

(continued)

Table 4-2. Studies of Nonbehavioral Family Intervention* (Continued)

Author	Research Adequacy	Sex-Age-Referral	Methodology	Exp'l N	Control/Comparison	Measures	Data Unbiased?	Follow-up	Outcome Findings
Donner & Gamson (1968)	*Inconclusive* Exp'l cases selectively chosen; no control/contrast group; variation length treatment; outcome criteria vague and biased; only 30% cases follow-up and criteria their selection not given; no control nonspecific treatment effects; data on which outcome conclusions re symptoms of IP not given; authors' conclusions that further therapy sought	–Male & female –13–17 –Referred as behavior problems	–Multiple family group therapy –Co-therapists: paraprofessionals without mental health academic credentials (Ph.D. in English & B.S.); received training –16 sessions planned; actually ran 10–30 sessions	N = 30 Families in 8 groups (plus 3 dropouts)	None	–Interview of 8 (30%) families by social work student re their perceptions of change –Improvement IP symptoms, in therapists' judgment	No No	"Several months"	–Of 8 followed, 7 reported improved communication –6 reported improved understanding other family members –3 reported improvement relations with IP –4 reported better insight –"Several" of the 8 followed up reported disappointment

					with therapy −20 (74%) IPs symptomatic improvement
by 44% of families with improvement is open to contradictory interpretation that this large proportion of families did not feel sufficiently helped			−Re-referral of IP to same agency	Yes?	−5 (19%) re-referred by schools, court −12 (44%) one or more members sought further therapy
			−Family/ members sought further therapy	No	

*Abbreviations used:

C: control or contrast group of cases; the group that does *not* receive the experimental treatment
E: experimental group of cases that *does* receive the experimental treatment
Exp'l: experimental
IP: "Identified Patient"; in these studies, the acting-out adolescent
N: number of cases (in experimental, control, or contrast groups)

Table 4-2. Studies of Nonbehavioral Family Intervention* (Continued)

Author	Research Adequacy	Sex-Age-Referral	Methodology	Exp'l N	Control/ Comparison	Measures	Data Un-biased?	Follow-up	Outcome Findings
	Inconclusive			Not Random					
Druckman (1979)	Defectors inadequate control/contrast group; 1/3 C group received alternate treatment elsewhere; no data on when recidivism measured; intervention so multiple that effects of any component cannot be discerned; no control nonspecific treatment effects; validity and/or sensitivity of Moos scale measure may be questioned; pre-	–Female –12–17 –Referred by court and probation as status offender	–Following 2-wk residential treatment of IP in which both girl and parents received melange of services (training in communication skills, "fair fighting," movement therapy, nutrition education, etc.) IP returned to parents' home and family seen in family therapy described as "goal-oriented" and "here-and-now"	N = 14 (plus 50 dropouts; 78% attrition)	N = 15 early dropouts (but 5 received non-family treatment elsewhere)	–Pre & post treatment; Moos scale of family cohesion, independence, organization. control	?	None	–At pre-test, neither E nor C groups had abnormal Moos test scores, indicating either normality of family functioning or lack of validity/sensitivity of measure –Post-test: Moos scores improved for both E & C groups; E scores not significantly different

Study							Recidivism		
		testing may have biased results of post-test; no information on therapists' competence; failures not explored	–Male & female	–8–12 sessions –2 therapists B.A. degree only; no information re training	N = 28 selected cases (plus 1 drop-out)	None	–Recidivism	Yes	Time period of follow-up not given	–No difference in recidivism E & C groups (50% each, discounting 5 hospitalized or incarcerated C subjects unavailable to commit offenses)
Kaffman (1963)	*Inconclusive* No control/contrast group; follow-up not all			–Short-term conjoint family therapy			–Therapists' clinical impressions	No		–Therapist and parent judgments

(continued)

Abbreviations used:

C: control or contrast group of cases; the group that does *not* receive the experimental treatment

E: experimental group of cases that *does* receive the experimental treatment

Exp'l: experimental

IP: "Identified Patient"; in these studies, the acting-out adolescent

N: number of cases (in experimental, control, or contrast groups)

Table 4-2. Studies of Nonbehavioral Family Intervention* (Continued)

Author	Research Adequacy	Sex-Age-Referral	• Methodology	Exp'l N	Control Comparison	Measures	Data Un-biased?	Follow-up	Outcome Findings
Kaffman (1963) Continued	cases; data not unbiased; any differences between therapist and parent judgments not described; no control nonspecific effects treatment	–6–15 –Referred for variety of problems including "disciplinary"	–Therapists: no information –Average 10 sessions but wide range			at termination –Parent report	No	6 mo (only some cases)	not reported separately –36% total improvement (symptom removal); 54% some improvement, 11% worse or no change
	Inconclusive Assignment to E or C group not random; intervention so multiple that effects of any one compo-	–Male & female –4–13 –Residential	–Intensive involvement family (minimum 6 hours wk in all aspects institution (meals,	*Not Random* N = 35 selected cases	N = 34 "traditional" service: family minimally involved	–Discharge placement at termination	No		–97% E group discharged to own home vs. 60% C group
Kemp (1971)									

126

				N	Outcome measures	Follow-up controlled?	Follow-up	Results
	nent difficult to discern; data not unbiased	treatment center; some children referred as "in serious trouble at home and in community"	school, outings, etc.) plus family therapy —Therapists social workers, psychologists, psychiatrists, or trainees in these disciplines. Other staff also involved with parents and child	$N = 55$ nonselected cases (but outcome data given on only 50 cases)	None	—and at follow-up	?	3 mo	—At follow-up same 97% E group still in own home vs. only 49% C group
	Inconclusive								
MacGregor (1962)	No control/contrast group; much variation length of treatment; data not unbiased; not	—Male & female —Adolescents —Referred	—"Multiple-impact therapy" with families in intensive format: 2-full days (20 hours)		—Therapists' impressions; —family's self-reports	No No		6 and 18 mo	—80% improved IP and family —6% no change IP

Abbreviations used:
C: control or contrast group of cases; the group that does *not* receive the experimental treatment
E: experimental group of cases that *does* receive the experimental treatment
Exp'l: experimental
IP: "Identified Patient"; in these studies, the acting-out adolescent
N: number of cases (in experimental, control, or contrast groups)

Table 4-2. Studies of Nonbehavioral Family Intervention* (Continued)

Author	Research Adequacy	Sex-Age-Referral	Methodology	Exp'l N	Control/Comparison	Measures	Data Unbiased?	Follow-up	Outcome Findings
MacGregor (1962) *Continued*	clear on how many families outcome is reported; no control nonspecific effects treatment	for behavior problem	–Team of 3 psychiatrists, 2 psychologists, 1 social worker; –Some cases received further treatment						but improvement family; –14% no change or worse both IP and family; –30% cases needed further therapy
MacGregor, Ritchie, Serrano, Schuster, McDanald, & Goolishian (1964)	*Inconclusive* No control/contrast groups; much variation length of treatment; data not unbiased; some cases receiving other therapy, so effects of exp'l	Same (6 cases schizophrenic; remainder behavior problems)	–Same (but notes that 11 IPs also in individual therapy elsewhere); –Same team, but with sporadic addition of a var-	N = 62 (outcome data on "half" of cases)	None	Same	No	9 & 18 mo (on half of cases)	–79% improved IP and family; –3% family improved but IP out of home

treatment cannot be discerned; shifting composition of treatment team; no control nonspecific effects treatment				iety of other professionals, e.g., trainees	−17% no improvement (no data on no change or worse) 11 IPs of successful group also in individual therapy, several parents also in other therapy at time of follow-up

Abbreviations used:

C: control or contrast group of cases; the group that does *not* receive the experimental treatment
E: experimental group of cases that *does* receive the experimental treatment
Exp'l: experimental
IP: "Identified Patient"; in these studies, the acting-out adolescent
N: number of cases (in experimental, control, or contrast groups)

(continued)

Table 4-2. Studies of Nonbehavioral Family Intervention* (Continued)

Author	Research Adequacy	Sex-Age-Referral	Methodology	Exp'l N	Control/ Comparison	Measures	Data Unbiased?	Follow-up	Outcome Findings
Menne & Williams (1975, 1976)	*Inconclusive* Cases selected, not random; no control group; no follow-up; no "hard" outcome measures (e.g., recidivism); objectivity of "independent raters" questionable; no information re therapists	–Male & female –Adolescent, most adjudicated delinquent but some predelinquent –Some institutionalized, some in other placements, some at home	–3 phases, separately reported, of 17-mo project evaluating family therapy with families of delinquents –1 site in institution for delinquents, 3 others community-based with co-therapist teams, qualifications not given –Much variation in intensity and duration therapy (2 to 20 + sessions)	Total N = 95 selected	None	–Therapists' judgments –Ratings of session audio- or videotapes by "independent raters" (project research consultant/author of report, and project director) –Families' self-evaluations –Jessness inventory	No Questionable independence of "independent" raters No Yes	None	–Very slight improvement

130

Study					Not Random or Matched				
Michaels & Green (1979)	*Inconclusive* Exp'l cases accepted as appropriate for family therapy, while C group were all cases seen in previous time period, thus nonequivalence of groups; different time frames of groups introduces further nonequivalence; no information on length of treatment of each group; outcome data possibly biased since same agency	–Presumably male & female –"Youths" –Referred as status offenders	–Family therapy in Minuchin-Haley model –Therapists: no information; received training –No information on length of treatment	N = 75 "accepted for family therapy"	N = 64 cases other treatment, seen in agency 2 yr before start of exp'l program	–Placements foster homes and institutions –Placement detention –Court action –Cost of placements	–? –? –? –?	At least 2 yr for C group; no information on follow-up time for E group	–Foster care and institutions: E 4% vs. 44% C –Detention: E 4% vs. 31% C –Court: E 4% vs. 33% C –Cost of placement E group only 18% that of C group

(continued)

*Abbreviations used:

C: control or contrast group of cases; the group that does *not* receive the experimental treatment

E: experimental group of cases that *does* receive the experimental treatment

Exp'l: experimental

IP: "Identified Patient"; in these studies, the acting-out adolescent

N: number of cases (in experimental, control, or contrast groups)

Table 4-2. Studies of Nonbehavioral Family Intervention* (Continued)

Author	Research Adequacy	Sex-Age-Referral	Methodology	Exp'l N	Control/Comparison	Measures	Data Un-biased?	Follow-up	Outcome Findings
Michaels & Green (1979) *Continued*	involved in placements; no information on length of follow-up or characteristics of therapists; no information on kind of treatment received by C group; no control nonspecific treatment effects *Inconclusive*								
Safer (1966)	No control/contrast group; cases selected, not random (but here this biases against, not for, positive out-	–Male & female –4–16 –Referred for aggressive	–Conjoint family therapy but individual therapy of child also in 13 cases. Both parents involved in only 8 cases	N = 18 selected as "inappropriate for individual therapy"; plus 11 dropouts	None	Unclear according to whose judgment, therapists or parents'/child's, data re symp-	No	4–16 mo	Outcome data includes 11 early dropouts –41% "successful"

132

(continued)

Study	Comments	Sample	Method	N	C	Outcome criteria	Follow-up	Controls	Results
	come); outcome data not unbiased; no control nonspecific treatment effects; no information on therapists; exp'l treatment confounded and variable	behavior; some on probation	−Family approach seen as second-best alternative for cases judged poor candidates for individual psychotherapy −Therapists: no information −8 sessions average			tom removal and reduction parent-child conflict		None	−21% some improvement −17% no change −21% outcome unrelated to therapy
	Inconclusive								
Schreiber (1966)	No control/contrast group; no follow-up; outcome data not unbiased; exp'l	−Male & female −X̄ for girls 12.5; for boys	−Conjoint family therapy in Satir model −Therapists: 11	N = 59 selected; plus 13 dropouts	None	−Therapist's judgments after 3 mo therapy	No	None	−56% symptom improvement

Table 4-2. Studies of Nonbehavioral Family Intervention* (Continued)

Author	Research Adequacy	Sex-Age-Referral	Methodology	Exp'l N	Control/ Comparison	Measures	Data Unbiased?	Follow-up	Outcome Findings
Schreiber (1966) *Continued*	cases selected, not random; failures not explored; no control nonspecific treatment effects	15 -Referred for behavior problems of children, also marital, economic, other problems	social workers, median 7.75 yr experience in individual therapy; received training family therapy -Sessions 1–12 mo, $\bar{X}$ = 4.3 mo, 12.8 sessions			-Therapists' judgments of 25 families in treatment beyond 3 mo	No	-92% symptom improvement	
Shaw, Blumenfeld, & Senf (1968)	*Inconclusive* No control/contrast group; unclear if cases random or selected; multiple interventions render effect of any one component difficult to discern; outcome data	-Male & female -4–16, 19% (44 cases) 13–16 -Referred for variety of children's	-Short-term therapy using variety of modes (individual, parent, and/or family sessions) -Therapists: "traditional team," no other	N = 227 unclear if random assign. or selected; 25% dropout; full data available on only 108	None	Therapist's judgment of: -Symptom removal/ amelioration -Parental attitudes	No No	12 mo	-Total sample much improved: 56% children, 62% parents -Of adolescents: 9.7% much improved; 35.5% some

Study	Sample	Treatment	Comparison	Measures	Controlled	Follow-up	Results
	problems	information –Limited to maximum 12 sessions in 3 mo		not unbiased; no information on therapists; no control nonspecific treatment effects	–Parent report of IP's symptoms — No –IP personality self-report — No –Therapist's observation of IP behavior in sessions — No	6 mo	improvement; 54.8% no improvement –29% much improved; –71% some improvement; –no cases worse/no change

Inconclusive

Study	Sample	Treatment	Comparison	Comments
Spiegel & Sperber (1967)	–No information on sex –No information on age; assume some adolescents –Referred for child problems	–Conjoint family therapy, not further described –Therapists: no information –6 sessions	None	Full report of study apparently not published; no control/contrast group; outcome data not unbiased; no control nonspecific treatment effects

Abbreviations used:

C: control or contrast group of cases; the group that does *not* receive the experimental treatment

E: experimental group of cases that *does* receive the experimental treatment

Exp'l: experimental

IP: "Identified Patient"; in these studies, the acting-out adolescent

N: number of cases (in experimental, control, or contrast groups)

(continued)

Table 4-2. Studies of Nonbehavioral Family Intervention* (Continued)

Author	Research Adequacy	Sex-Age-Referral	Methodology	Exp'l N	Control/ Comparison	Measures	Data Un-biased?	Follow-up	Outcome Findings
Sigal, Barrs, & Doubilet (1976)	*Inconclusive*			*Not Random or Matched*					
	Outcome data not unbiased; low follow-up response rate; groups not random or matched; no control nonspecific treatment effects	–Male & female $\overline{X}$ = 9.7 but some adolescents –Referred for variety of children's problems including behavior	–Family therapy, insight-oriented, nondirective –Therapists mostly psychiatric residents, also staff psychiatrists, psychologists, social workers –At least 3 sessions, $\overline{X}$ = 47 wk	N = 62 (out of 161) response to follow-up mail questionnaire, so 39% response rate	N = 31 (out of 71) response to follow-up mail questionnaire, so 44% response rate	–Parent report re IP symptoms; satisfaction with family functioning	No	4½ yr	–E: 74% improved vs. 77% C –E: 18% no change vs. 8.5% C –E: 7% worse vs. 8.5% C (Differences not significant) –E significantly more new symptoms: 44% vs. 13% C –Nonsignificant difference in family functioning: E 57% improved vs. 39% C

**Abbreviations used:*

C: control or contrast group of cases; the group that does *not* receive the experimental treatment
E: experimental group of cases that *does* receive the experimental treatment
Exp'l: experimental
IP: "Identified Patient"; in these studies, the acting-out adolescent
N: number of cases (in experimental, control, or contrast groups)

136

Jayaratne (1978) broke down communication skills into components of interruptions, the length of time individual members dominated family conversation, and the time it took the family to arrive at mutually acceptable decisions. His contracting/communication training intervention package resulted in improvement in interruptions and decision time but no change in dominance patterns as measured by the length of time one member controlled family conversation.

The results of Alexander and Parsons still stand, and are considered seminal in research of this kind of intervention. They have, however, never been totally replicated. All that can be said at present is that this type of intervention does seem to show great promise, but further empirical support is necessary.

FAMILY TREATMENT OF DELINQUENCY FROM A NONBEHAVIORAL PERSPECTIVE

Nonbehavioral family therapy studies do not lend themselves to an easy delineation of the particular type of family therapy or the specific techniques involved. In contrast to the behavioral family research, which usually reported quite specifically just what the intervention consisted of and what observable changes it was hoped would result, with a few exceptions the descriptions of the nonbehavioral family projects are vague about precisely what it was the professionals *did,* and specifically what changes *in what posited variables* the intervenors hoped to bring about.

We have rather arbitrarily grouped the studies of nonbehavioral family interventions into (1) those that focused on change of family interactional processes; (2) those that utilized a short-term crisis family therapy model; (3) those with a clearly psychodynamic focus on expression of feelings and insight development; (4) those that worked with multiple-family groups; and finally, the largest group of studies, (5) those in which the intervention can best be described as "eclectic" or where it is not described at all.

An argument could be mounted that the two studies of Ferreira and Winter (1966, 1968) and the study by Haley (1964) should more properly be considered behavioral intervention, since these investigators focused on changing very specific aspects of family communication. However, they did not describe what the "family therapy" consisted of, and there is no evidence that it was behavioral in theoretical perspective or technique. In all three studies, the families involved were tested at the end of 6 months of therapy, and no appreciable or significant changes were found.

The "structural" school of family therapy of Minuchin (1967, 1974) and Haley (1976, 1980) was tested in a 1979 study by Michaels and Green with families of adolescent status offenders. Good outcome was claimed, but no real conclusions about this type of family intervention can be drawn because of the deficiencies of the research design and execution. The cases that received family therapy were selected, not randomly assigned or matched; the "control" group was nonequivalent in that it consisted of cases that had received regular (non-family therapy) services from the juvenile corrections system 2 years earlier; and the outcome data concerning youngsters who were placed in institutions or foster homes or who received further court action are biased in that the professionals involved in the treatment seemed also to be in control of these kinds of case dispositions.

Short-term family crisis intervention was studied by Baron and Feeney (1976), who claimed reduction in further court actions and detentions; but since the family therapists involved were probation officers who were responsible for case dispositions, the same caution concerning the nonobjectivity of the outcome data applies as for the Michaels and Green study discussed above. The same may or may not apply to the Beal and Duckro project (1977), as it is not clear from the report if the family therapists were also the adolescents' probation officers. If they were not, then the findings possibly indicate some effectiveness of the family therapy utilized, but other methodological flaws in this study render the findings "inconclusive evidence."

Byles and Maurice in 1979 studied the impact of short-term crisis family therapy provided by a community mental health agency to 154 families with a delinquent youngster. Only 70 families accepted the offer of the special service. When these were compared with a contrast group who received the traditional Police Youth Service Bureau services, the findings indicated an *increase* in further law violations for the experimental group. Families who accepted treatment had a higher recidivism rate (69 percent) than those who refused the experimental service (57 percent), although this difference was not statistically significant.

Spiegel and Sperber (1967) researched the impact of crisis family therapy with 7 cases seen for six sessions. Outcome, according to the Leary Interpersonal Checklist, parents' reports, and therapists' observations, indicated improvement. Defects of the research design, however, render the usefulness of this research report "inconclusive".

The psychodynamic school of family therapy is represented by five studies. Sigal, Rackoff, and Epstein (1967) studied the correlation of therapists' prediction of outcome to actual outcome in 19 selected (not randomly assigned) cases. Outcome data were not free of possible bias since the judgment of improvement was based on the clinical opinion of senior staff members rather than on more objective criteria. However, the findings indicated that although no families were considered to be totally improved, approximately three-fourths experienced some improvement, and one-fourth were the same or worse. Therapists' earlier predictions of outcome were not correlated with the outcome perceived by the senior staff.

Postner, Gottman, Sigal, Epstein, and Rackoff (1971) reported on a smaller subgroup (N = 11) of Sigal and associates' larger sample. The focus of this study was on the relationship between case progress (if treatment had not yet ended) or outcome (if treatment had terminated) and family interaction patterns audiotaped at intervals throughout treatment. Poor outcome seemed to be related to such family interaction variables as a highly involved, verbal mother and a passive father, and to such therapist variables as passivity and tendency to focus on the more talkative parent rather than on the family as a whole.

Wellisch, Vincent, and Ro-Trock (1976), in working with a hospitalized population that appeared to include some nonpsychotic adolescent behavior problems, found no clear changes in the client group that received psychodynamically oriented family therapy on their measures of communication and problem solving. However, rehospitalization rates and length of time between discharge and return to work or school were appreciably lower for the family therapy group than for a comparison group in which only the adolescent received individual therapy.

The Satir (1964) model of family therapy was studied by Schreiber (1966). Judgments by the therapists indicated improvement of the client group, but the nonobjectivity of these data plus other research flaws render this study not a valid test of the Satir approach.

Sigal, Barrs, and Doubilet (1976) conducted a follow-up study, an average of 4.68 years later, of families who had received nondirective, insight-oriented family therapy, compared with follow-up data on cases who had early dropped out of treatment. The response rate to follow-up questionnaires was low, and the only significant difference of the treated group from the defector control group was that the family therapy cases had *more* new symptoms!

Garrigan and Bambrick in 1975 and again in 1977 tested Zuk's "go-between" technique of family therapy. Findings were so mixed that it is difficult to arrive at overall conclusions.

MacGregor (1962) and MacGregor, Ritchie, Serrano, Schuster, McDanald, and Goolishian (1964) studied "multiple-impact family therapy" as a treatment modality. In this approach, the family is seen individually, in different dyads and triads, and as a group by a team of therapists for several full days in succession in a highly intensive format. The first study by MacGregor reported on the outcome of 50 families, and the study by MacGregor and his associates in 1964 reported on 62 cases. Like the Tharp and Wetzel study (1969) reported under behavioral interventions, the research component seems not to have been planned for in advance but rather "tacked on" post hoc, rendering the findings of improvement in 79 to 80 percent of the families difficult to assess. Further, a number of the families had one or more members in treatment elsewhere, either concurrently with the experimental therapy or subsequently, but before follow-up data were gathered, thereby making it impossible to factor out the particular impact of the independent variable of multiple-impact therapy.

Group therapy of families was studied by two projects. In 1968, Coughlin and Wimberger used this technique with 10 cases "arbitrarily selected" by the therapists (i.e., neither randomly assigned nor matched) from a waiting list. In addition to the multiple-family group, some cases also received treatment in individual family therapy, a parents' group, and/or a children's group, thus making it impossible to determine the effectiveness of any one component of the treatment "package." At termination, 8 families reported improvement, but 2 of these requested further therapy, and the professionals recommended continued therapy for 3 more families—meaning that only 3 families were considered both by themselves and the professionals to have been sufficiently helped that further therapy was not indicated. A mail follow-up at 6 months brought responses from only half of the treatment group; of these 5, 4 felt helped (but in 3 of these families the troublesome adolescent had moved out of the home). The only conclusion that can be drawn from data like these is the Scottish verdict "not proven."

Two paraprofessionals, Donner and Gamson (1968), also tested multiple-family group therapy. The quality of the outcome data here was slightly more objective than in the Coughlin and Wimberger study: a social work student interviewed 8 of the 30 families that had been treated (but since the student was dependent on the agency for a passing grade in her field practicum, her objectivity might well be subject to argument). Of the families followed up, several reported having more insight or improved understanding of other family members, but only 3 of the 8 felt their relationship with their troublesome adolescent had improved. These findings belie the authors' claim of the efficacy of their treatment.

"Other" family therapies: the remaining 12 studies can be classified only as "therapy not described" other than that it involved the family. Evans, Chagoya, and Rakoff (1971) conducted a study that looked not at outcome per se of family treatment of hospitalized adolescents and young adults (some of whom included nonpsychotic acting-out teenagers) but rather at what kind of families were given the opportunity by the therapist to become engaged in family therapy and how this correlated with case outcome. Of 100 cases, half were offered family therapy by the therapist assigned to the patient, but half were not, despite an agency policy that all cases receive family therapy as well

as individual therapy for the young patient. The clinical judgments of the therapists involved indicated superior results for the cases that had received family therapy, somewhat supported by family reports that agreed with the professionals' judgment in 66 percent of the cases. An interesting finding of this study was that those cases that were offered family therapy were initially healthier (which of course explains some of the outcome data) and were from a higher socioeconomic bracket.

Ginsberg (1977) tested a "relationship enhancement program" for fathers and sons with 14 volunteer dyads (who, however, did not necessarily have problems). Audiotaped communication interchanges between the fathers and sons and audiotaped unobtrusive observation of their interaction indicated some impact of the experimental treatment. It is not clear, however, whether the therapist was the judge of the audiotapes, which of course could compromise the objectivity of the data.

Maskin and Brookins in 1974 studied the impact of counseling focused on parent-child interaction during a 4-month aftercare program after discharge of delinquent adolescent girls from a residential program. Outcome data indicated significantly *higher* recidivism rates for girls living with both natural parents as compared with subjects living with a single parent or in a foster home; this may be considered surprising, unless it is viewed as possible evidence both of the negative impact of a troubled home setting on the adolescent and also of the difficulty in changing such a family. In 1976 Maskin studied the impact of individual and group counseling, also focused on improving parent-child interaction, with 30 male adolescent delinquents while in a residential corrections program and again four months after discharge. The experimental group was matched with a similar group that did not receive this kind of counseling. The cases that received the experimental treatment demonstrated a recidivism rate of 17 percent as compared with 77 percent for the contrast group (but length of follow-up before recidivism was measured is not given).

The remaining eight studies fell so short of meeting commonly accepted standards of research methodology that their findings are not useful. Reliance on therapists' impressions only (e.g., Cutter & Hallowitz, 1962; Safer, 1966; Shaw, Blumenfeld, & Senf, 1968), treatment that consisted of such a melange of therapies that the effect of any one intervention cannot be assessed (e.g., Druckman, 1979), biased outcome data (e.g., Kemp, 1971), and otherwise inadequate research design and execution (Menne & Williams, 1975, 1976, 1976) confound the results reported and preclude the possibility of reaching meaningful conclusions.

CONCLUSIONS: RECOMMENDATIONS FOR FURTHER RESEARCH DIRECTIONS

The evidence of this group of studies concerning the impact of various types of intervention with the families of delinquents is generally more suggestive than conclusive. A few conclusions of the "harder" variety can, however, be attempted.

There is no evidence whatsoever that nonbehavioral family therapy is effective with the problem of juvenile delinquency, regardless of the "school" of therapy utilized (e.g., systems, structural, psychodynamic, strategic, communication, crisis, multiple impact, and so forth). The only reports of effectiveness are to be found in the poorly executed research studies; the better the research design and implementation, the more likely is it that a finding of ineffectiveness emerges. Nonbehavioral family therapies may be effective with the problem of delinquency, but this needs to be demonstrated by empirical evidence that to date does not exist.

If the proponents of nonbehavioral family therapies wish to establish the validity of their theory and techniques, then the responsibility is theirs to expend as much time and effort in better research as they do in theorizing and technique development.

In contrast, while behavioral interventions with the families of delinquents have also not been demonstrated to be totally effective, the evidence so far is tilting the scale in their favor. Nonbehavioral family therapists appear to have less interest in and capability for research than their behavioral colleagues, despite the fact that research courses are required in the training programs of most of the mental health professions. It may be that (in contrast to behaviorally oriented training programs) research is not taught in such a way that it is perceived as relevant to and integratable with clinical practice (Wood, 1978). Clinical instructors tend to teach their professional students theories and techniques of practice without attention being given to whether empirical evidence exists for their effectiveness or to the responsibility of practitioners themselves to develop such empirical evidence as an integral part of their practice.

Despite this criticism, it is of special note that behaviorally oriented family interventions, according to the evidence of these studies, were most successful when they incorporated some of the nonbehavioral systems perspective of the family therapists. It would appear that, despite the quite different philosophies and theoretical underpinnings of the two camps, they have something to offer to each other and, in some areas at least, can be integrated into an intervention model (see, for example, Birchler and Spinks [1980], for an account by a mental health clinic of their attempts at such an integration). The behavioral school, it would seem, has something to learn from the family therapists about process variables. A narrow "behavior only" perspective may tend to render the therapist oblivious to such other factors in organizational family life as role assignments, mutual expectations of family members, power distributions, perceptions of the disciplinary and executive role of parents, and so on. These indeed should be reduced to operational, behavioral terms; it may not be easy to do so, but it is potentially possible. Not all behavioral practitioners recognize that when they succeed in changing, for example, the behaviors of parents and children, they have in effect changed not only behavior but interactional *process* as well. It is as important to focus on and to study systematically such variables as it is to maintain a precise frequency count of child behaviors. Systems family theory may help behaviorists to take a broader perspective; but since behavioral theory is more molecular, it in turn may help family systems theory to become more operational (and therefore, ultimately less vague and abstract)—theory more in the middle range and thus more pragmatically applicable to better interventive technique.

It is also possible (as some research studies on the outcome of psychotherapy have found) that the particular theory espoused by the practitioner is not all that important. What may be most important may be the practitioner's ability to assess accurately the most relevant and salient factors operating in the problem that are potentially changeable and then to direct focused interventive effort at these factors, resisting sturdily all temptations to become sidetracked by the clients' fascinating but irrelevant material or by the practitioner's own theoretical biases.

However, the studies examined here all started not from careful case-descriptive examination of the nature of each of the families as individual units and their differences from each other, but from the theoretical bias of the clinicians/researchers. What was tested in most of the studies was a technique, not the kind of plan of action to fit individualized situations that one would expect from professionals in other disciplines—medicine or plumbing, for example. It is possible, nevertheless, that buried under the mountain of data of all this research is an indication that since most of the studies helped some families and failed with others, the successes were cases that fit the theoretical Procrustean bed set up for them, and the failures were those that found that bed ill-designed for their specific needs.

Despite the inadequacy of the research designs in many of the studies to serve as a support for their authors' claims of glowing success, it is not unreasonable to speculate that even the worst-researched projects did indeed help *some* families and youngsters. The problem with the research designs is that neither the authors nor the reader can account for the differential results. Our speculation might continue that behaviorally oriented intervention helped families who needed this kind of help with specific skills and failed with families who needed something else; whereas family systems therapists were helpful to families who needed to change something in the structure or process of their family organization and failed with families who needed something else.

Although research purportedly focuses on the null hypothesis, researchers are human, and there inevitably and understandably is a sense of disappointment and failure when the emotionally dear experimental hypothesis fails confirmation under rigorous test conditions. When we are dealing with matters as complex and ill-understood as "the family" and "delinquency," however, we need not only to be prepared for failure but also to expect it (if not to welcome it, which would be beyond human capacities) and to be prepared to learn from it. Failures alert us to what is deficient in our theory and our technique armamentarium and thus lead to their refinement and improvement (Popper, 1972). But none of the projects considered here went on to study who were their failures and why the clinicians (not the families, certainly) were the ones who failed.

There is inevitably a dilemma involved. Practitioners cannot behave as tabulae rasae with each new case. They will be ineffective if they cannot bring some theoretical cognitive map to aid in sorting out and drawing inferences and conclusions from the mass of case data with which they are bombarded. The dilemma is that there is also real risk involved: the practitioner is almost driven to a dedication to the *one* theory that seems to him or her to resolve the felt cognitive dissonance, the contradictions, the gaps, the case data that just won't fit neatly inside the theoretical cage. We do not seem to be doing an especially good job in helping students in the several helping professions to come to grips with the inevitability of the "holes" in knowledge and the lack of certainty.

In other mental health areas we are beginning to recognize that we are dealing with phenomena that are better called "the alcoholisms" rather than alcoholism, and "the schizophrenic disorders" rather than schizophrenia. If the practitioners in the studies reviewed here are representative of practitioners generally in the field of juvenile delinquency, it seems clear that the field needs to move away from a monocular and reductionist view of delinquency to a recognition that what we are dealing with is a heterogeneous phenomenon. The practitioner wedded to psychodynamic theory cannot assume that every delinquent needs insight therapy; the practitioner with a dedication to family system theory cannot assume that every family of a delinquent needs strategic—or paradoxical or whatever—interventions to change the structure and process of the family; the behavioral practitioner cannot assume that every family needs only to be taught contingency contracting.

A useful assumption from which to initiate future outcome research is that we cannot expect to find *the* breakthrough intervention that will work for every delinquent and every family; that what we will find is some success and some failure—and that *both* success and failure then need to be examined closely to bring us nearer to the answer to the essential question of what treatment delivered by what kind of helpers works for what kinds of people experiencing what problems under what life- and service-delivery circumstances.

Descriptive research is needed to establish differentiations among the various kinds of families that can have a delinquent child, to serve as the empirical base to undergird intervention theory. That intervention or prescriptive theory will then be in a better position to be developed and refined, and especially to *differentiate* which kind of families need what kind of intervention. The small descriptive research project conducted by the authors and reported in Chapter 3 is a small and preliminary example of this kind of descriptive research. Developing this knowledge base is such an important next step in the quest for effective intervention in juvenile delinquency that it might be recommended that it be given top priority as a research strategy, a higher priority certainly than continued outcome studies of intervention. Without the necessary data base concerning delinquents and their families, the probability is that further studies of this type will continue to yield mixed and inconclusive results, since the interventions employed are not individually and differentially selected to fit the needs of different cases.

Descriptive research is also needed that focuses on how "ordinary" families (i.e., families with no more remarkable pathology than is to be found in any family) deal with problems and crises such as the delinquent behavior of their youngster. Pathology cannot be used as a negative template for health, since health is a more positive quality than the mere absence of dysfunction. All families (like all individuals) are dysfunctional at least for temporary periods and/or concerning particular stresses or life tasks and problems for which their previously developed coping capacities do not prepare them. The turmoil of adolescence is such a stress for most families. But many, and probably most, individuals and families not only recover from but gain valuable learning and expansion of their coping repertoire from having struggled through the problematic situation—and not necessarily with any professional help at all. What are the processes that these families have learned and that outsider professionals do not yet know but that we might learn from them?

Lane and Burchard (1983) in their review of a range of behavioral interventions that have failed to modify delinquent behavior relate the success or failure of a program to four variables: (1) the characteristics of the service provider, (2) the characteristics of the youth, (3) the characteristics of the intervention program, and (4) the interaction of these three variables (p. 371). We suggest adding two other critical variables and addressing the interaction of all of them:

Characteristics of the service provider.

Characteristics of the youth.

Characteristics of the family.

Characteristics of the material and social environment of the youth and family.

Characteristics of the intervention program.

The interaction of all five variables.

1. A body of research literature substantially supports the fact that the personal characteristics and interpersonal skills of the intervenor—whether a behavioral or nonbehavioral approach is being used—are some of the most important variables in successful outcome. Additional research is needed to examine further the specifics of these variables: one such specific in which we are particularly interested is whether the intervenor's attachment to a par-

ticular theoretical perspective focuses his or her attention to only selected data in the case.

2.   In their review of behavior modification failures with delinquency, Lane and Burchard (1983) conclude that two variables concerning the youthful client can be identified as relating to the success or failure of delinquency intervention: "the age of the youth, and the extent to which the youth has been involved in delinquent behavior . . . [T]he treatment of choice for the younger, predelinquent, or status offender should involve family-behavioral intervention with a focus on the modification of inappropriate family interactions" (p. 372).

These authors recommend for the older delinquent an intervention package combining high school equivalency diploma tutoring and job placement. These services would undoubtedly be important for the older adolescent who has dropped out of school and is unemployed and whose subsequent boredom, frustration, and lack of money may thereby predispose him/her to further delinquency. The family of the older adolescent is usually not in the same position of control as the family of the younger child, so that interventions that set as a goal the parents' assuming control of the youth's out-of-home behavior may indeed not be reasonable or achievable. We would argue, however, that it would be a mistake of intervention strategy not to include the family in the intervention plan, which in the case of the older adolescent has a different but still crucial role to play in terms of its influence, its support, and its monitoring of the youth's utilization of the other services made available to him/her. For the older adolescent living at home, it may be the interactive effect of interventions focused both within and without the family—by the family and by the professionals—that will synergistically permit any one component of the intervention to be effective.

3.   Research-based knowledge concerning family characteristics that appear to be related to acting-out and

delinquent behavior on the part of children, such as we summarized in Chapter 2, is growing slowly. Much more descriptive research needs to be done to provide a more solid base for interventive theory.

4.   Most of the research reviewed in this chapter focused on one or a few of the above variables. The variable that has consistently been ignored is the environment and its characteristics. If the individual cannot be understood without also understanding what his behavior means in the wider context of family vectors, then neither can family behavior be understood without understanding what that behavior means in the wider context of community, cultural, and other social-ecological factors that are some of the forces requiring the family to behave as it does. None of the studies looked at what the reality was like for their delinquents and families in the specific surroundings of neighborhood and community; work and economics; the quality and quantity of school, recreational, and other community facilities; wider societal forces such as the drug culture, racism, and sexism; and, in 1986, a political policy that is not supportive of minorities, the poor, single parents, and adolescents in their developmental struggle.

5.   The clear evidence that seems to emerge from this examination of the relevant research is that *nonfocused* family interventions, i.e., those that address themselves vaguely to encouraging communication in general or expression of feelings, are totally ineffective in the treatment of adolescent delinquency. At present, despite the lack of similar findings in attempts to replicate the studies that demonstrated the most positive effects, the impression is that the kind of intervention employed by Alexander and his associates (1973, 1976, 1982), which combined focused efforts to change selected family interaction patterns with behaviorally oriented contingency contracting between parents and adolescent, holds the most promise for this client group. Several suggestions can be offered, however,

for the direction of future research concerning the intervention variable itself.

First, research designs need to attempt to build in ways of studying both the separate and the synergistic effects of a family-change and a behavioral intervention. Second, even the more highly focused family-change efforts of the family-behavioral programs (at least more focused when compared to psychodynamic or other nonbehavioral family therapies) are still not specific enough. More extensive and intensive *descriptive* research is needed to identify the particular factors in such areas as (a) family interaction patterns generally, (b) the specific role relationships of parents and adolescent and between the parents as a marital-parental subsystem, (c) the influence of the sibling system, (d) the positive or negative impact of grandparents and other extended family, (e) differences between nuclear and single-parent and step-families. Data on these questions might throw some further light on the issue of the family's role in the etiology of delinquency, but much more important, they will help us better to understand (a) the ways in which the family might become caught up in behavior that unwittingly perpetuates its member's delinquency (analogous to the helping efforts of the wives of many alcoholics, who are inadvertently thereby preventing their husbands from taking responsibility for their drinking problem) and/or (b) the specific resources and latent strengths of the family-as-a-group and its individual members that might be mobilized in the attempt to help the delinquent to change his/her self-destructive behavior.

6.   The sixth variable cannot be researched unless and until more data are accumulated about the separate impact of the first five. But one of the reasons that this group of research studies yields such contradictory and/or incomplete and/or soft data is that the *interactive* effect of characteristics of therapist–delinquent–family–intervention techniques and program–environment is not known. This

is not to fault the studies examined. Since the basic descriptive and other research has not yet been done, we are
still a long way from being able to answer the bottom-line
question, "What interventions, by what kind of helpers,
with what kind of delinquent clients, in what kind of families, in what kind of social circumstances, are the most effective and efficient?"

Chapter 5

PROBLEM ANALYSIS AS THE BASIS
FOR INTERVENTION

We have several times characterized juvenile delinquency as a phenomenon that is not homogeneous, not unitary, not simplistic. It is therefore essential that an individualized analysis of why the delinquency exists be conducted in each case, to form the basis for an individualized and differential choice of the intervention or interventions needed. What seems to happen in many agencies, or at least what did happen in many of the agencies that reported their practice research efforts, is that the practitioners have their minds made up in advance about the diagnosis of why delinquency exists in a given family, and are equally committed to a particular intervention—before they even meet the young offender and family. There are serious ethical issues involved in the superordinate position given to the theoretical belief system of practitioners over the rights and needs of clients, including their right to be listened to and to have their situation objectively assessed, with problem-solving measures individually and differentially selected to match that assessment.

Given the present popularity of family therapy, it is not surprising that this is the modality now most frequently offered by many community agencies. But family therapy is a treatment approach oriented to changing the structure and process of the family organization. An agency's commitment to family therapy as its singular stock-in-trade means that the agency has decided, *in advance of ever seeing the clients,* that something amiss in family structure or process is what is causing the delinquency. Our study of delinquent families, however, indicates that by no means is this always so. Delinquency can occur in families in which there is nothing particularly wrong at all with their structure and process. Or delinquency can occur in families in which the organizational structure and process are seriously skewed and dysfunctional, but for whom either the prognosis for a family therapy approach is poor or the family flatly refuses this form of treatment. And then there are some families that can be demonstrated to need, to be able to benefit from, and to accept a family therapy intervention approach.

This, of course, also applies to agencies and practitioners with a vested interest in behavioral treatment approaches. Not every family has a delinquent adolescent as a result of the parents' poor parenting skills or ignorance about how to contract with the youngster for behavioral change. ("Contracting," of course, as useful as this technique is *for those families who need it,* is not something invented by behavior modification psychologists; parents have been doing this for millennia, although they have used more homely terms to describe it.)

Similarly, agencies and practitioners who are committed to a psychodynamic explanation of all of their clients' problems in living will tend to see insight-oriented therapy as needed by every delinquent. Only some, but by no means all, delinquent adolescents have emotional disturbances of the type that psychodynamically oriented individual therapy might help.

Assessment, pyschosocial assessment, or *diagnosis* are the terms most often used by professionals to describe their process of attempting to figure out what they are faced with in a given case, what the problem in the case is all about, and what factors—causative, contributory, perpetuating, or exacerbating—are sustaining the problem. We prefer the term *problem analysis* because it seems to describe more simply and clearly than do the older terms the nature of this analytic process.

The multiplicity of factors and forces that are involved, in different combinations and permutations, in each individual case might be sorted out into three major subsets or dimensions:

(1)   the adolescent him- or herself (the intrapersonal dimension);
(2)   the family (the interpersonal dimension);
(3)   the environing context in which both youngster and family exist (the dimension of the physical, social, and economic environment).

THE ADOLESCENT

The family therapy movement developed at least partly, and perhaps largely, in contravention to the monocular focus on the individual alone of the then-prevalent psychodynamic ideology. Some schools of family therapy now appear to consider the individual as if he/she existed only as a member of a family system, with no internal life or motivations private from the family, with no life outside the family and no external forces also impinging upon him or her. Rather, it may be hypothesized that individual adolescent delinquents may be found somewhere on a continuum as described below. The individual delinquents studied in the small descriptive research project reported on here, as well as those studied in previous investigations by other researchers, do seem to sort themselves out on such a typological continuum; but it must be emphasized that the continuua suggested here concerning individual adolescents, and later concerning the family and the environmental context, represent no more than a preliminary first-draft attempt at a conceptual typology.

1. The "normal" adolescent, or "boys will be boys," delinquency syndrome: no marked intrapersonal pathology, no major complicating personal difficulties as in 2.

2. Still a "normal" adolescent in terms of absence of marked intrapersonal pathology, but personal difficulties exist for the youngster that make it harder for him or her to deal with adolescence, peers, family, school, and the outside world, e.g., intellectual deficit, problems with physical health or appearance, and the like.

3. Some intrapersonal pathology that cannot, however, clearly be associated with the need to commit delinquent acts. (An individual can have a broken leg *and* a head cold at the same time; simultaneous occurrence or occurrences briefly separated in time do not in themselves supply evidence of cause and effect.)

4. Intrapersonal pathology that can reasonably be causally related to the delinquent behavior (e.g., rage, need to strike back, and so on) as correlated with delinquent acts that at least provide face validity of expressing these upset emotions.

5. Adolescents suffering from very severe psychological disturbance or psychosis (although it should

be noted that psychotic young people, although they sometimes commit crimes such as Hinckley's attempted assassination of President Reagan, do not predominate as a diagnostic category among all juveniles who commit delinquent acts).

6. The true "sociopath"—a very ill-understood diagnostic category but one that does seem to exist, although such individuals are fortunately rare.

The following three cases provide an illustration of the different types of adolescent behaviors that come to be labeled as delinquent.

Case No. 1: Robert Gomez

Robert, age 15, has been arrested once for possession of marijuana with intent to sell and for assaulting the police officer who attempted to arrest him and his friends. Robert denies both charges, claiming that it was his friends who both had the marijuana and who threw a bottle at the police officer. He admits, however, that this peer group in his former neighborhood were "not good kids" and that they did drink beer and smoke pot together; but he claims that since his family moved to their new neighborhood he is no longer associating with them and no longer smokes marijuana, although he does drink beer occasionally.

Robert is the youngest of four children of Puerto Rico–born parents, with brothers aged seventeen and eighteen and a sister of sixteen. None of the older siblings has been involved with law violation. All three, however, despite their young ages, are married; one brother is out of the home, but the other two siblings live in the parental home with their spouses and the infant children born to both young couples. Despite having only two bedrooms for nine people, the apartment is neat and the furnishings give evidence of pride in its appearance. The parents are in the process of buying the two-apartment home (the other apartment provides income) in an older residential section, now multiethnic, with evangelical storefront churches interspersed among the homes, but in a relatively quiet and respectable neighborhood.

Robert's father works in a factory. His mother is not employed, as both she and the father feel strongly that her place is in the home. The father is also perceived as the decision-maker and authority: he gives detailed instructions to his wife every morning before leaving for work about particulars of running the house. Both parents see the family as their center, having few activities outside the home with the exception of visiting with mother's brother and sister who live nearby. Robert is reportedly also close to this aunt and uncle and their families. Additionally, at least some members of the family try to return to Puerto Rico for a visit once a year to see grandparents there.

The father is proud of Robert's prowess as an amateur boxer and wrestler, often shares this activity with him in the house, and says he would one day like to be his son's manager if Robert takes this up seriously. There is a boxing program at the local YMCA, which Robert talks of joining although he has not yet done so. The family usually has dinner together, although the father sometimes eats alone in the living room "to get some peace and quiet." The mother defers to her husband during interviews. Although his English is good, hers is more limited and she uses family members as interpreters.

Both the eighteen-year-old married brother in the home and the equally young husband of Robert's sister are unemployed although looking for work. Mr. Gomez says he knows it would be better for the young couples to have their own homes, but he is not looking forward to having them and his grandchildren move out.

The father believes that Robert's mistake was in getting mixed up with the wrong crowd, who scapegoated him by leaving the scene, letting him take the blame. He is co-operative with the probation officer but does not perceive any particular role that probation can play other than its mandated duty of checking on Robert every so often. The father takes on the responsibility to stay in regular contact with Robert's school to monitor the boy's performance, which is passing, although Robert does not like school. The family does not belong to any organized religion and has no contact with other community agencies.

Although one may or may not buy the youngster's and the father's account of the incident that resulted in Robert's arrest, there is no evidence to suggest that the boy is at risk of recidivism. There is no evidence *from the data of the case* of intrapersonal pathology. Robert's adaptation to school is probably not markedly different from that of most of his Hispanic and black age-mates in this inner-city school. However, the strongest evidence to buttress a prediction that the delinquency will not be repeated is the nature of the family system. Some practitioners might perceive individual and/or family pathology in the father's very active involvement in every aspect of family life and the mother's seemingly passive and submissive role. But these roles and dynamics are characteristic of Puerto Rican culture (see, for example, Garcia-Preto [1982]); and the case evidence seems to indicate that whereas such roles may not be acceptable to and would not work for college-educated, sexism-liberated, non-Hispanic families, they are working for *this* family. (It should also be noted that in the Puerto Rican family, the mother is a good deal more powerful than superficial observation would indicate.) The family's relative isolation from their environing community is also not uncharacteristic, and it does not mean that the family is socially isolated; their social world is the extended family, and that is a very active social world.

The most positive prognostic indicator in this case

would seem to be *the family's sense of its role as a primary "therapeutic agency" for Robert.* They perceive probation as helping them, not as their helping probation. All of the data in this case point to a decision for minimal professional intervention. The family seems to be handling the situation quite well, better than the professionals can. Pending further data to indicate that the adolescent and/or family need more help, the role of the professional should be restricted to supporting the family's efforts with their son.

Case No. 2: Thomas Lane

Thomas, a fourteen-year-old black youngster, is on probation as the result of "wayward and incorrigible" charges brought by his mother. When he was three, his father died of an overdose of heroin. The mother is reported also to be a drug abuser and to have had a series of relationships with other men, even when her husband was living. After his death Tom and his older brother were shuffled back and forth between their mother and the paternal grandmother. Tom began truancy from school, and open conflict with his mother about his behavior and his dislike of her most recent boyfriend led her to bring the charges.

Charlie, the twenty-five-year-old brother of Tom's dead father, offered to have Tom live with him. The mother consented and granted Charlie legal guardianship of his nephew.

Also with the young uncle is his adopted son, Tom's thirteen-year-old cousin Alvin. Alvin's unmarried mother felt burdened by having to support nine children and offered to let Charlie adopt Alvin, which he did 1 year ago.

Charlie is the only sibling in his own large family to graduate from college. He is employed as a counselor and music instructor at a local community recreation and service center for inner-city youth. Charlie is active in his church, but since the boys are not enthusiastic about religion, Charlie requires them to attend with him only every other Sunday, giving them a Sunday off for their own pursuits on alternate weeks.

Alvin was somewhat jealous when Tom arrived, but Charlie feels that the boys get along quite well now, and they share household duties. After school, the youngsters go to the community center where Charlie works, since he feels that Tom especially should not be unsupervised. All three sometimes eat dinner together at the center, or the boys go to the home of their paternal grandmother (the mother both of Charlie and of Tom's deceased father), where Tom's brother now lives. Since Tom spent much of his younger years back and forth to this grandmother, he is reported to be attached to her and sees her and his brother usually every day. Other siblings of Charlie's live in town and are involved as extended family.

Charlie is firm about rules, responsibility, and cooperation in household chores. But he also says he thinks kids need to "let off steam" once in a while. He and Tom have spent a lot of time discussing Tom's feelings about his parents and about leaving his mother. Since the move to Charlie's home and his assumption of legal guardianship took place only recently, it is not known what role Tom's mother will play in future.

Charlie and the boys live in a third-floor apartment on a quiet residential street in a predominantly black and Hispanic area of the inner city. The house needs some repair, but the apartment, while somewhat cluttered, gives evidence of effort spent to make it attractive and clean. Each youngster has his own bedroom.

Charlie's salary is adequate to maintain the household of three and to support his interest in music (he plays several instruments). No information is available concerning his personal social life.

Because of excessive truancy earlier this year while he

was with his mother (he missed all but 18 days of the term), Tom will not receive credit for this academic year and will probably have to repeat the grade next year. He does not enjoy school because he realizes he will have to repeat eighth grade. Charlie stays in close touch with the school to monitor Tom's attendance and school work. So far the boy has not been truant.

This youngster might be expected to be more emotionally scarred than Robert Gomez in the preceding case. What is surprising is that he is not more so; and it can be speculated that the presence in his life of the young uncle, his grandmother, brother, and other extended family is what has made the difference for him.

The nuclear group of Charlie, Tom, and Alvin is certainly not a traditional family, but it is definitely a family. In addition, Tom is very clear that he still has a brother; although they do not live under the same roof, they see each other every day. The focal grandmother continues to loom large in both their lives.

The young uncle, only twenty-five years old, appears to be quite competent in his parenting skills. Certainly he does not need to be taught "contracting" or other behavioral techniques. At his age, however, Charlie can be considered quite young to take on the responsibility for rearing two troubled and rejected teenagers, despite his experience with adolescents on his job. The emotional scars created by Tom's earlier life may or may not be within the young uncle's capacity to deal with by his caring, provision of a family life, and commonsense handling of his "sons." It is possible that Tom might need and could benefit from individual therapy focused on his reaction to his mother's rejection. For now, however, there are insufficient data to support a decision that this is definitely needed. Uncle Charlie is at present handling the situation quite competently; until and unless further data are developed that indicate the need for professional intervention, it would seem that efforts of professionals should be restricted to support of the created and extended family as the primary rehabilitative resource.

At his age Charlie should have a need for a personal social life, and lack of information about this is an important diagnostic datum that the student researcher missed. A cynical observer might wonder whether he is homosexual and if sexual interest in the boys explains his motivation. But there is no evidence of this; and his religious values, professional interest in teenagers, and commitment to family provide adequate competing explanations. If Charlie marries or forms another adult attachment sometime in the near future, the boys could be expected to react negatively to a competitor for his attention and love. Charlie may need some professional help if this comes to pass— or he may indeed handle it quite well himself.

Case No. 3: Eddie Marciano

Ed, age seventeen, is the youngest of six children in an Italian-American family. His first involvement with the law was at age twelve for assault; since then, there has been a string of other charges of further assaults, fighting, motor vehicle moving violations, assaulting a police officer, malicious damage, and perhaps arson. At age ten he became a concern to the school because of his behavior and poor academic performance. He received neurological evaluations (the findings of which, however, are unknown). His IQ has been tested as dull normal. A psychological evaluation found him to be "severely impulsive and anti-social," and referred to a further unspecified "serious disorder" for which it was predicted he might need psychiatric hospitalization in the future. He is completing high school in a special school for emotionally disturbed children because the regular public school could not handle him. He has worked in an auto body shop and in construction but is unemployed at present.

Ed is described as "huge" in body build, with a shuffling gait. He is usually rather dirty.

Ed's female probation officer likes him, referring to him as an "overgrown teddy bear" who has a "tender inner core" beneath his tough exterior. He talks to her about his problems and admits that his behavior has been wrong, but says his temper is so bad he can't help himself. Ed is reported also to have a good relationship with the guidance counselor at his special school.

Ed was born to his parents, now aged fifty-eight and fifty-seven, late in life as the last of their six children, the next youngest of whom is 7 years older than Ed and the oldest 20 years older. None of the siblings has ever been involved in law violations. All are married and out of the home but living in the same state. A sister once contacted the probation officer to ask about the possibility of a group-home placement for Ed, since she was worried that he would eventually end up in jail. Ed refers to himself as the "bad apple" in the family barrel. He spends most of his time outside of school hanging around a local pool hall with his buddies. It is not known whether the peer group also is involved in delinquency.

Ed's father supported the family as a junk dealer before his serious heart condition forced him to retire. He received Social Security disability payments for a time but for some reason has been declared ineligible now. The family currently receives Aid for Families with Dependent Children (AFDC), which will terminate when Ed reaches eighteen. The father appears to be limited intellectually and is quite deaf.

Ed's mother is even more deaf than her husband, and her speech is blurred to the extent that question has been raised as to whether this might be a congenital or very long standing communication deficit. She also appears to be of limited intelligence. She did not know the name of Ed's school or where it was located.

The parents are isolated except for visits to their married children and grandchildren. The mother is close to her sister, but there is little contact with the father's family. The probation officer feels that the parents, because of their deafness and limited intelligence, are "not tuned in to the real world." Ed treats his parents gruffly and disrespectfully, and they appear to be afraid of him.

Living conditions for the family are marginal: their poverty is evident in their small apartment over a bar in an industrial/residential area on a major noisy highway. The apartment's rear entrance is reached by a hazardous, rickety flight of wooden stairs. Furnishings are old and worn but adequate and clean.

Certainly Ed must be considered a very disturbed young man, at high risk for recidivism. The comparative seriousness of his past offenses, the early age at which they began, their repetitiveness over time, plus his limited intelligence and the psychological report findings point to an almost certain likelihood that he will erupt angrily again.

The parents are older than their years, limited intellectually themselves, isolated, and afraid of and realistically incapable of dealing with their hulking, contemptuous, angry son. They need help with their own quite severe health and economic problems and their social isolation; but it is unrealistic to set an intervention goal of helping them to deal more firmly and effectively with Ed. Unlike the cases of Robert Gomez and Thomas Lane, the Marciano parents cannot be considered a primary rehabilitative resource for their son.

But there is an extended family: five adult siblings of Ed's, at least one of whom was concerned enough about him to contact his probation officer. Could any one, some, or all of these brothers and sisters provide for Ed the acceptance and interest in him that his parents cannot give and the external structure and controls that he lacks internally? Would it be possible for him to live with one of the siblings? If so, the other siblings need to be as much involved as possible: Ed is a very difficult young man, and the sibling group would need help to become the effective family system for him. One major intervention by the professional would therefore need to be directed at the substitute family of the sibling group.

There is no information available about the nature of Ed's relationships with his brothers and sisters, other than the brief note in the probation record of the telephone contact by his sister. But there is evidence, from the nature of his relationships with the probation officer and the school counselor, that Ed can relate to caring people and that he is perceived as likeable by people who take the trouble to find out who he is. The siblings may not perceive him this way, or for other reasons may not be motivated, or their own individual life situations may prevent their taking on responsibility for him. If they cannot, then the second-best and only remaining chance for Ed would be a group-home substitute family.

Because Ed can relate and does respond to a caring professional relationship, and because he obviously needs professional help with his inner turbulence that family members cannot be expected to be able to provide, he also should receive supplementary individual therapy.

THE FAMILY

As individual adolescent delinquents cannot be seen to be homogeneous, the families of delinquents are not homogeneous either: they are more likely to be different from each other in important respects than they are to share exactly the same kind of intrafamily dynamics. The field needs to develop better diagnostic understanding of the *different* kinds of families who have delinquent children, in order to apply triage principles to the selection for intervention of those families in which normal processes of recovery from adolescent delinquency will not occur.

It might be hypothesized, for example, that families of delinquent adolescents will be found on a continuum similar to that which we suggested for the individual delinquent adolescent. Although our research families did seem to sort themselves out on a continuum such as that we present below, the same caveat applies: this is a preliminary first attempt at conceptualization of a differential typology.

1. "Normal" or well-functioning families that are able to deal with their youngster's transitory delinquency and that need no professional intervention other than possibly information, provision of community resources, and/or help with environmental pressures but that definitely do need support of the parent(s)' handling of their child and of their efforts to "de-label" him or her as a delinquent.

2. Families in which the parent(s) would be able to function as adequate executives in an "average expectable environment" but that are realistically unable to deal with massive negative forces that are having an impact on their adolescent and themselves (e.g., actively antisocial norms of the peer group or neighborhood); and/or parents who are so burdened by the struggle to survive and provide for their families under conditions of such social pathogens as poverty and racism that they are not able to expend the energy necessary to attend to their teenager's needs.

3. Families in which the parent(s)' previously learned parenting skills are good but in which new skills need to be learned to deal with an adolescent child at a normal life stage of rebellion, identity search, and need to risk him- or herself outside the home to establish a sense of personal mastery and/or to win approval from a peer group.

4. Families in which the youngster's acting-out is symptomatic of disturbance in family structure and process, e.g., in which the child has been forced to undertake parental responsibilities, or has been pulled into a coalition with one parent against the other, or is acting out a submerged family conflict.

5. Families in which the parent(s)' parenting skills have never been good and who need intensive skill training.

6. Families that just do not have the capacity, even with professional help, to deal with their adolescent any differently or better (e.g., the Marciano parents); or families that socialize their children to antisocial norms (the criminal family).

The following cases represent some of these divergent family types.

Case No. 4: John Forte

Seventeen-year-old John, white, has been expelled from three public schools for selling drugs, truancy, and disruptive behavior; he flunked out of an expensive private school. John is on probation as a result of incorrigibility charges that his father brought after the boy became angry at not being able to find the keys to the father's car, attacked the caretaker on the family's estate with a pitchfork, and damaged the property with a tractor. Since he has been on probation, he has consistently violated probation rules, which his parents do not report for fear that he will be sent to an institution.

Mrs. Forte was born in Scotland to a poor family and came to the United States as a young adult. Her husband is the American-born child of a large and equally poor Italian family.

Even though the couple did not have any children for the first 10 years of their marriage, both Mr. and Mrs. Forte preferred that she stay at home. They had never investigated the reason for their infertility but decided to adopt John's now twenty-year-old sister Jane when she was three weeks old. Four years later they adopted fifteen-month-old John. The couple was unwilling to discuss any questions having to do with their sexual adjustment on the research interview protocol, with Mr. Forte brushing aside any inquiries remotely related to that topic.

Mr. Forte is a self-made millionaire, and he uses this term proudly to refer to himself. He owns more than a dozen different businesses, in which several of his and his wife's relatives are employed. The family lives in a large, beautiful home on 45 acres with a spectacular view.

The interaction between the parents gives evidence of a very close and mutually supportive relationship. Mr. Forte moved a hassock beneath his wife's feet during the interview to make her more comfortable. When discussing painful issues concerning John, they consoled each other with a pat on the hand or a neck rub. Yet they claim to be very different temperamentally and credit this difference with being the successful ingredient in their marriage. Mr. Forte is a self-proclaimed "Type A" person: ambitious, high strung, emotional, a workaholic. He could not remain seated during the interview for more than a few minutes at a time. Despite having had a heart attack 4 years ago, he is still a heavy smoker.

Mr. Forte dresses flashily, his wife much more conservatively. Also in contrast to him, she has a calm, "laid back" manner. When her husband became excited during the interview, she calmed him by reaching out to pat his hand. The difference in their personalities leads to separate interests and activities: Mr. Forte's recreation is casino and horse gambling; his wife is active in golfing, several women's organizations, and the Catholic church. Most of their mutual friends are business related. Mr. Forte says he does not have any close friends other than his wife. The couple has several times attended church-sponsored marriage encounter groups, the philosophy of which they find helpful in keeping their marriage so satisfying.

The affection evidenced between the parents is not, however, demonstrated in their relationship with their children. Both children interrupt the parents and make derogatory side remarks while the parents are talking. At one point John told his mother to shut up. The parents cannot understand this behavior, citing that they have always given the children everything they asked for. The children, however, are unimpressed with what they call their parents' "phony generosity," and John complained that his father never spends time with him. Mr. Forte recently changed his will to remove John as a beneficiary; when asked about this, he answered rather matter-of-factly, "Well, in case he or his friends plan on doing away with me for my money."

John and his sister are close, talking with each other a great deal about their plans, details of their respective romantic activities, and their feelings about being adopted. They are especially united in their negative perception of their parents. The parents had previously handled any difficulties with the children with another purchase or promise of a trip, but this no longer works. John's and Jane's rebellion is now open and concerted: they refuse to eat with their parents, refuse to do chores, and blatantly violate home rules and regulations. They refuse to go to church with their mother and consider themselves atheists.

Jane is not employed, although she is thinking of going to a fashion school. She spends her days at home and goes out every night. Jane feels that she is entitled to "freedom" now after graduating from her boarding school. She admits to use of marijuana and alcohol at parties but denies other law violations.

John was evaluated at a community mental health center on referral from probation. The recommendation was family therapy, which the children and mother were willing to try but the father refused: "I don't believe in that stuff." Mr. Forte now regrets having brought the incorrigibility complaint, as he fears that the probation department may send John to an institution as a result of his repeated infractions of probation rules. He seems to have signed the complaint out of desperation and to want to forget that fact now that John is on probation. Mr. Forte is contemptuous of John's probation officer and feels she doesn't know what she's doing.

The diagnostic evidence seems clear that John's destructive eruption that brought about the incorrigibility charges by his father was only one expression of his (and his sister's) sense of emotional deprivation, under their "spoiled rich brats" exteriors. The dynamic on which the marriage appears to operate is the mother's skill and willingness to serve as a walking bottle of tranquilizers for her neurotic husband. What Mrs. Forte gets from the relationship besides the obvious returns of feeling needed and appreciated, and having her affluent life style provided, is not clear; and perhaps these satisfactions are indeed enough. What does seem clear is that the dynamics of the marital relationship leave no room for others, including children. The children seem to have been added to the couple's physical life space in the same way as they might have purchased a couple of paintings to add to their art collection.

The prognosis for helping this family as a group would depend on the existence of a more positive sense of commitment and caring on the part of the parents than is evident so far from the bleak facts of the case. The mother is to a large extent an unknown quantity, and there may be more emotional depth than is apparent under her cool blandness. She did state she would have been willing to try family therapy. But despite his neuroticism, his egocentrism, and his resistance to help by outsiders, the father may be more reachable than he appears: the mother may be hurting about her kids but she doesn't show it—and he does. "Joining" him, in the parlance of family therapy, at the level of his basic dynamic of needing to see himself a strong, good, and especially a successful man may win entry for a skilled practitioner.

Even if this more optimistic picture develops as a result of additional data gathering, the prognosis for real change at a family level would still seem poor, since basic change would require a shift in the marital equilibrium that neither partner seems to be in a position to permit.

The student research interviewer on this case failed to develop data about extended family, although a fairly large one does exist. Have the children had any kind of close relationship with a grandmother, an aunt, or uncle? Are the extended family members employed by Mr. Forte so intimidated by the fear of losing their livelihood that they could not risk his displeasure? Would he indeed see such a relationship of his children with other family members as a threat, or perhaps as a relief from responsibility? The fact that no other relationships like this were mentioned may indicate that they were never allowed to develop, and at Jane's and John's ages it may not be practicable to attempt to build them now.

Failing restructuring family therapy as an interventive strategy or helping John to use a substitute parent in the form of an extended family member, behavioral contracting is certainly worth a try. Mr. Forte, as a successful businessman, knows all about making deals, and the "deals" involved in contracting should appear to him sensible and helpful, without the threat of their being labeled "therapy." A behavioral contracting approach could reasonably be expected to improve somewhat the severe and stalemated conflict between parents and children, but of course it would not do anything about the children's realistic sense of rejection and deprivation. Individual relationship therapy for John might help him to deal with the reality of his family in less destructive ways.

Case No. 5: Steven Corto

Steven, age twelve, was arrested for breaking and entering with a group of other youngsters.

His mother is the child of an Oklahoma rural minister; his father is one of 15 siblings in an Italian-American family. The young couple received much financial and emotional support from the father's family in the early years of the marriage. The mother now takes responsibility for the breakup of that marriage, describing herself as very young, spoiled by all the attention and help of her in-laws: "My husband couldn't do enough, couldn't make enough money to satisfy me." Two older siblings to Steven were born: a sister Deborah, now twenty-one and married; and Salvador, now eighteen and living with his father. When the mother was pregnant with Steven, the parents separated. Mr. Corto challenged his paternity of Steven and has never accepted the boy as his. The parents were divorced when Steven was two months old.

The next several years for this family read like a badly plotted soap opera. When Steven was less than a year old,

Mrs. Corto married a man from South America with limited English, who had trouble keeping a job, stayed out nights, and gave no help with the children. They moved to his South American country about a year later, where the mother was isolated and unhappy because of the language barrier. She gave birth to a baby girl who died several months later from multiple birth defects, whereupon her husband left her. The mother returned to the United States and subsisted on welfare for several years. Her first husband reentered the picture to "kidnap" the two older children, taking them with him to a distant state. Despite her efforts she could not get them back and ultimately stopped trying. Her letters to the children were returned unopened by the father. Last summer, however, her now twenty-one-year-old daughter came to visit against her father's wishes to show her mother her grandchild.

Mrs. Corto said she had many relationships with men during this period, most of them unhappy. She felt her life was over and that she had failed at everything. Her welfare caseworker suggested she take a licensed practical nurse course, and Mrs. Corto identified this as a turning point for her. She obtained a night nursing job in a local hospital, which she likes and where she is considered competent.

Mrs. Corto became friendly with her brother's best friend, David, a young man 12 years her junior. At first she considered herself his "big sister," and when she found herself having sexual fantasies about him, she became so upset and guilty that she entered psychotherapy at a community clinic. Six months of therapy convinced her that there was no basis for her guilt, so she initiated a sexual encounter with David that she says "is the smartest thing I ever did in my life." One week later David moved into the home.

David is self-employed in a home repair and construction business, and the couple's combined incomes are adequate for the family needs. Their relationship seems compatible and affectionate. Mother credits David with "sharing the load—the responsibilities of the house and rearing Steven." David describes her as "mature, loving, someone I can learn something from." When observed together, there seemed to be real affection among the family members, with a great deal of mutual touching.

Steven considers David his father, and there is a close relationship between the two. David thinks that active sports involvement is the best deterrent to a boy's getting into trouble and points out that the time Steve did get into trouble with his friends was between baseball and football seasons. Steven has won "Player of the Year" and other awards for his sports prowess. His stepfather is very involved in the boy's sports activities.

Steven is expected to do his homework after school before he goes out; he has reasonable curfews and is punished for infractions by losing TV privileges. Neither parent considers him a discipline problem. Steven admits to making a mistake in his involvement with the law but claims he was not fully aware of what the group of boys he was with that night were planning to do. The parents feel that the boy showed poor judgment but is "basically a good kid." The mother has worked with him on his school work, which has improved from all C grades to B in some subjects.

The family goes camping together frequently. They have no contact with extended family on either side since these relatives disapprove of their unmarried status. Although mother says she is in no hurry to get married after having been "burned" twice, the student researcher had the impression that she does indeed want to marry David but is waiting for him to bring up the subject and is fearful of seeming to pressure him.

The family rents half of a large house in a pleasant

suburban community. A large vegetable garden is maintained in the yard. The furniture is attractive, standards are good, and the atmosphere is cheerful and lived-in.

Steven was evaluated at a local mental health agency, where he was found to be a "normal healthy adolescent—no treatment needed".

If one did not look carefully at the detailed data of this case, it would be easy to jump to conclusions that one or another type of professsional therapeutic intervention was needed, merely on the basis of the youngster's offense, or the mother's past unstable history, or the mother's and stepfather's inability to make a legal commitment to each other, or the difference in their ages.

Some might have concern over whether the relationship between the mother and David will endure, since he is only twenty-four to her thirty-six years and since neither partner has been able to make a commitment. One wonders what will happen as the stepfather matures, requiring a shift in the basis of the marital relationship. But how these factors will work themselves out in the dynamics of this specific marital relationship is unpredictable at the present state of knowledge of any of the helping professions or of the social and behavioral sciences that underpin them. Stranger marriages (or marriage-like relationships) have indeed survived and flourished. What seems important for the delinquent youngster at present is that the parental relationship and the family do seem to be working now. Further, both mother and stepfather are caring, responsible, and involved. They do not excuse Steven's behavior but see it as the result of his youth and poor judgment and perceive him as a basically "good kid"; i.e., they are de-labeling him as a delinquent without condoning delinquent behavior. Their disciplinary and other parenting skills appear to be good, and they need no help with these. If there are rocky shoals or a shipwreck ahead for the parents, then professional help might well be needed. But in the interest of the principle of the least intrusive and most parsimonious intervention, the actual data of the case would seem to indicate an intervention plan for the present that focuses only on supporting the parents' own efforts.

Case No. 6: Dennis Kelly

Dennis, age sixteen, is on probation for alcohol possession and possession of marijuana with intent to distribute. Parents describe him as having been no trouble when he was younger, doing good school work and active as an altar boy and in sports. When he entered the large suburban public high school, he "got in with the wrong crowd," his grades plummeted, and he became involved in drinking, smoking pot, and staying out late.

Mrs. Kelly was born in Ireland, one of 11 children. Her father is now deceased; her mother still lives in Ireland but frequently visits several of her children who are in the United States. Mrs. Kelly came to this country at age eighteen to live with an aunt.

For the first 20 years of their married life, Mr. and Mrs. Kelly, to whom four children were born, lived in an apartment in the home of his parents. Mrs. Kelly developed a close relationship with her husband's mother, and although the father-in-law had a drinking problem, both parents recall this period as helpful to them, financially and in terms of the support and companionship of the extended family. After 20 years of saving for a down payment on their own home, the couple were able to purchase their own small tract home 3 years ago; they consider this a "step up." The neighborhood is respectable, although the street is noisy and affords little privacy. The house is slightly cluttered but clean and adequately furnished.

Mr. Kelly's income as a printer is adequate for the family. Mrs. Kelly had worked as a telephone operator before her marriage but since then has not been employed, as both she and her husband feel her place is with the home and the children.

Mr. Kelly had an increasingly severe drinking problem for the past 6 years, which caused much family stress and emotional estrangement between the parents. Several months ago he was detoxified in a residential center and has not been drinking since. He attends A.A. meetings "occasionally," but the family has never been involved in AlAnon or other programs. Although the mother feels her husband is usually "quiet and kind," he has a "vile temper" when drunk. Mrs. Kelly seems resigned to the fact that their relationship can never be as close as it was in the early years of their marriage, because of the distance that developed between them when he was drinking, and she credits her religion with giving her the strength to deal with this reality.

Mrs. Kelly is very much the spokesperson for the family, with her husband seeming to be uncomfortable in expressing himself. The student researcher had the impression that painful topics are glossed over in the family, and that a premium is placed on not exposing feelings or troubles to each other or to the outside world. For example, only the older sister knows of Dennis's trouble with police; the two younger children have not been told nor has the extended family.

Both partners were uncomfortable with questions about their sexual adjustment. Since they have never practiced any contraception other than the Church-approved rhythm method, sexual relations have always been infrequent. All of the children were conceived despite the use of rhythm, but the parents say they would not have spaced them any differently, since they feel each child's conception was ordained and blessed by God.

Mr. Kelly spends several evenings a week bowling and bar visiting with friends (although he now sticks to soft drinks). With the exception of visits to the extended family, the family does not share any activities together out of the home. Each individual seems to have his own life.

Mrs. Kelly is a bubbly, energetic, affectionate woman. She frequently leaned forward to touch the interviewer's arm during conversation. She hugged the eleven-year-old youngest son, showed concern about the recently injured arm of the fourteen-year-old boy, and when not in contact with the younger children, she stroked the family dog. She admits to being "incurably affectionate" and feels that "a child can never get enough loving." But she finds it easier to be demonstrative with the younger children than with sixteen-year-old Dennis, his twenty-year-old sister Mary, or her husband. She describes her husband as much less affectionate, since he feels that this makes a boy a sissy. When he left the room at one point, Mrs. Kelly whispered to the interviewer that her husband has a terrible time relating to the children, intimating jealousy on his part. Since his drinking problem developed 6 years ago, he does not get involved with their activities anymore and has "given up" on Dennis because of his getting into trouble. "This is my cross to bear." Mrs. Kelly is intensely involved in her religion. She makes a remark about God's will or God's grace in almost every sentence and frequently refers to her church group activities.

At the mother's behest, regular attendance at Sunday Mass was made a condition of Dennis's probation. Although she hopes he will do well in school, religion is a more important value to her than education.

Shortly after the imposition of probation the parents transferred Dennis to a Catholic high school to remove him from his peer associations at the public school, even though the tuition at the parochial school is a financial hardship. Dennis was initially unhappy at the new school. When his mother learned he had contacted his old friends, she reported this to the probation officer, who issued a warning.

Gradually, however, the boy made new friends, acquired a girl friend, and ended the school year with a good attendance record and a C average. He obtained a part time job at a local gas station, which the mother considered "the best thing that ever happened to him."

The younger brothers are both described as quiet, studious, and no problem. Since Dennis's trouble with bad companions at the public school, the parents plan to transfer these children also to parochial school. Sister Mary lives at home and is employed. She participates little in the life of the family, keeps to herself, and refuses involvement in Dennis's problem.

Dennis may never become involved again in law violation, but he might be considered as at risk of developing alcoholism like his father at some time in his life. He is a lonely, emotionally constricted boy whose family is not sufficiently available to him. His father ignores him, and although his mother cares about him, she has little understanding of or skill in dealing with the needs of an adolescent male. The parental-system dynamics assign her sole responsibility for his delinquency. Although she has taken action in terms of changing Dennis's school and monitoring his behavior, basically the mother is fatalistic, seeing his "straightening out" as the product of prayer, not family action.

This family seems never to have "worked" at any better than a marginal level, because of the father's exclusion from family life and the mother's preference for a relationship with God to a relationship with her husband, as well as her religiously inspired fatalism about her ability to influence events that she feels are essentially a matter of Divine Will (see, for example, McGoldrick [1982] concerning the dynamics of the Irish-American family). This marginality was probably adequate when the children were young; but as they have gotten older, each family member seems to be centrifugally spun out into individual, isolated orbit. The mother is the only centripetal force in the family, but her perspective of her role is not such that she can hold the group members together when the early childhood stage is passed.

It may well be possible to help this family via a restructuring family therapy approach that focuses on encouraging the father to take on more of a role in a parental team concerning the children, that helps the mother to deal with the fact that she will have to seek other life "employment" than her role of mother as the children grow up, and that helps the parents to address some of their marital issues. Parental training in the different parental skills needed in dealing with adolescents, of which both parents seem to be ignorant, would also seem to be needed.

It is distressing that when trouble in the family surfaced as a result of Mr. Kelly's alcoholism, the response of the professional helping system was restricted to him as an individual. No one seems to have recognized that the alcoholism meant also that the *family* was in trouble. Given the data in the case concerning the father's isolation and his emotional estrangement from his wife and children, it is difficult to be optimistic about the father's ability to maintain sobriety. Indeed, everyone in the family seems to be terribly lonely, needing each other but not knowing how to reach out. They are all so needy, and their basic commitment to each other seems strong enough, that the Kellys could probably be considered a good bet for intervention targeted at these factors.

Case No. 7: Billy Archer

Billy, a white boy aged fourteen, has a long history of maladjustment and law violation. He was expelled from kindergarten for hurting other children, later tortured small animals, and at age ten bit another child so severely that plastic surgery was required. At eleven he threw a knife at another youngster, at twelve he threw rocks at other children and at cars, at thirteen he stole flares from a car and set fire to the woods behind the family's home, and a few months ago he committed the offense for which he is on probation—threatening his family with a hatchet and sexually assaulting his brother and sister.

Billy's father declined to be interviewed by the student researcher. He has worked in the same factory for many years, and Billy's mother sees his ability to hold a job and his abstinence from alcohol as his most outstanding characteristics. According to his wife, he has no friends and prefers to keep to himself. Mrs. Archer also likes to be left alone, so this poses no difficulty. Her only complaint about her husband is his contradiction of her discipline of the children. She does not know his reaction to Billy's most recent offense since "I never asked him."

Mrs. Archer is grossly overweight and dirty. She has a limited vocabulary, with the exception of swear words, and has marked difficulty in expressing herself. She seemed unable to comprehend even simple concepts. There is evidence, additionally, of a thought disorder. She believes she has psychic power over Billy and that this is why he doesn't like her. When she became pregnant with her first child, she refused to accept this diagnosis, being convinced rather that she had a tumor; she went from one doctor to another trying to find one who would agree to remove it surgically. She had much trouble with the births of all three children because "they tried to come up out of me instead of the other way out."

Sister Annie, seventeen, is described by the mother in the girl's presence as "a little retarded." She dropped out of school last year and is not employed. She is grossly overweight. Annie ran away from home twice, once to accompany a motorcycle gang and the second time after the sexual incident with Billy, but she is not on probation.

Brother John, sixteen, is also overweight. The mother calls him "my strength—without him I would die." She keeps him out of school frequently to be with her. As a result, he is failing all subjects and has been referred to the school psychologist.

The family never eats meals together, all members preferring to obtain their own, usually from a fast-food outlet. Evenings are spent in front of the TV with apparently little interaction among the family. They occasionally visit one cousin who seems to be the only extended family member available, but usually weekends are spent in individual pursuits.

The mother relates to the children in a hostile, abrupt way. When the daughter came into the kitchen to get something to eat, her mother screamed at her to "get the hell out of here." She is openly rejecting of Billy. The three siblings fight constantly, and the mother took the student researcher on a tour of the house to show her the marks of violence everywhere: puncture holes in the ceiling from a stick, all three bedroom doors kicked in. Housekeeping standards are filthy, which the mother excuses on the basis of her bad back and Ménière's disease, which causes a constant ringing in her ears.

The neighborhood of small tract homes is adequate, but the Archer home stands out like a sore thumb in that the exterior of the house is as dilapidated and uncared for as the interior.

The family has been seen for evaluation at a mental health agency, where Billy was diagnosed as suffering from nonpsychotic organic brain syndrome. Family therapy was recommended but refused. Billy was later examined again at a specialized evaluation center, where he was diagnosed as sociopathic personality. He was placed in a group home where, however, they could not handle his behavior, and he was transferred to a residential treatment center where he remains.

This is not a "criminal family" in that they do not actively promulgate law violation as a norm, but they are the closest to this category of all of the families studied. The mother is clearly psychotic, and father is no paragon of mental health either. If mother would consent, psychotropic drugs might help her somewhat, but it is not realistic to expect enough change in the parents or the family to salvage the other children by any treatment approach currently available. Removal of the children from their psychotogenic family would seem to be the only option, despite the legal difficulties that might be associated with this. It is difficult to understand why the school system never brought a charge of child neglect to the state child welfare agency, although such a charge could probably be substantiated without difficulty. It is also difficult to comprehend why the judge in Billy's case merely placed him on probation, until his continued acting-out required placement out of the home. The controlled residential setting in which Billy currently lives is clearly the only option for him at present, although it is difficult to be optimistic about his prognosis or his future. Quite aside from the controversial issue of a possible genetic component in some types of psychosis, the damage done to Billy by spending his developmental years in this crazy, uncaring, and violent family environment can be, at best, only partially remediable.

THE ENVIRONMENT

Just as the individual adolescent cannot be understood fully unless he or she is seen in the context of the family, the family cannot be completely understood unless it is seen in its social, physical, and economic milieu. The environment is a variable in all situations of delinquency, with greater or lesser import for the problem itself, but always a variable that needs to be taken into account.

1. At the most positive pole of a continuum is the "average expectable environment": not perfect in terms of material provision, not without stresses and pressures of various kinds, but sufficiently supportive that the family is enabled or at least not impeded in the performance of its tasks.

2. As the environing context becomes less supportive in terms of income, housing, service resources, and a sense of community in which the family is accepted and contributory, so does the family's ability to perform its tasks become more difficult.

3. At the most negative pole are environments that are hostile, depriving, dangerous, and/or actively inculcating of prodelinquency norms—such as are found in some inner city slums.

The Gomez family (case no. 1, pp. 159–162) is an illustration of the impact of a poor neighborhood, poor community services, and a delinquency-prone adolescent culture. Indeed, in the Gomez case, the influence of the latter variable looms larger in the genesis of the youngster's delinquent conduct than do either intrapersonal or family variables.

In other situations, the picture is more mixed, as illustrated by the following cases.

Case No. 8: Henry Nelson

Henry is a fifteen-year-old black male on probation for participating with his peer group in extorting money from another youngster.

His mother, age forty-three, was born in North Carolina to a very poor sharecropper family with many children. Twenty years ago she moved with her two children to an inner city in New Jersey, where three more children were born. No father seems to be in the picture, and Ms.

Nelson is unwilling to talk about her children's father or fathers.

The mother was employed as a housekeeper in a local hospital but lost this job when she attempted to move back to North Carolina. The move was unsuccessful, as she could not get work there, and she returned to New Jersey. All of the mother's brothers and sisters also now live in New Jersey. Although she is on a waiting list to get her old job back at the hospital, her income is now AFDC. The mother is involved in her local church, for which she is a missionary; this provides her only contact with her neighbors. She says that she has learned that "short visits make good friends," and she prefers this minimal contact.

Also in the home is Henry's sister Barbara, twenty-one, a high school dropout, unemployed because at present recuperating from surgery to remove a tumor. Sister Rhonda, seventeen, is also unemployed and cares for her four-year-old child; she was a high school honor student before she also dropped out of school. A twenty-three-year-old sister living out of the home is currently on probation. Brother James, nineteen, is serving a sentence in the state reformatory for robbery. Also in the home for the past year is the seventy-five-year-old maternal grandmother; the student researcher failed to develop information concerning her, and her relationship with the family is unknown.

Henry is doing passing work in school and finds the sports activities offered there and at his Boys Club "exciting." His mother has gone to watch him play at basketball games. She hopes the probation officer will be able to persuade him to stay out of trouble, but in view of the police difficulties of her other children she seems rather hopeless about this.

Henry denies ever having used drugs. He also claims he was not involved in stealing the money for which he was charged; rather, his friends gave him $10 that they, not he, had taken from another youngster. He earns money from his paper route, and last summer worked in a local CETA program.

Housing is adequate though crowded for the seven people: a three-bedroom apartment in a two-family house in a rundown section of this old city. Furnishings are worn, but housekeeping standards are adequate.

Henry must be considered at risk for future delinquency, primarily because of the history of law violations on the part of the other siblings. His mother cares about him and goes to watch him play in basketball games. But the family history of law violations by siblings must raise the question as to whether this never-married and isolated mother, with no opportunities for her own self-fulfillment, struggling apparently largely alone (the role of grandmother and extended family elsewhere in the state is not known) to survive in the face of welfare-status poverty, lack of education, societal racism, and the like, can realistically be expected to protect Henry against the pressures of his delinquency-supporting peer group and the turmoil of adolescence. The Gomez family (case no. 1) also has to struggle against racism, a somewhat better but still marginal income for their large family, and several others of the pressures that beset the Nelson family; but the Gomezes appear to have more going for them—primarily their family solidarity and mutual support; their clear roles (which, if not acceptable to everyone as a life style, at least give the individuals involved a solidly based sense of who they are, what they are worth, and what is expected of them); and an active social and support network of extended family. The role played by Ms. Nelson's mother and her siblings needs to be explored; perhaps they are more of a resource for her than the record indicates. If they do not now serve this function, the professional then needs to explore if they can be helped to do so.

But the evidence of the incarceration and the probation status of the two older children and the pregnancy at age twelve of the younger daughter, as well as the mother's isolation and her inability to get off welfare, seem to indicate the need for an intervention plan that emphasizes supporting the mother, building a support network for her from the extended family, and teaching those specific parenting skills concerning her adolescent that she seems to lack. The family lives in a rundown, delinquency-prone neighborhood with some, but not sufficient, community services; social action advocacy on behalf of all of the Nelsons at risk in this environment would seem to be as necessary an intervention as direct efforts with the family.

Case No. 9: Larry Carter

Larry, a sixteen-year-old black youngster, is on probation for purse snatching and for participating with his brother in auto theft.

Larry's parents divorced 6 years ago. His father contributes financially to the family "when he can," but he is currently unemployed. He lives in the same town and sees his three sons about once a week.

Mrs. Carter had worked as a nurse's aide in local hospitals for many years. Although she is only thirty-five years old, she has diabetes and a heart condition severe enough that a physician recommended she stop working. Several months ago she took in a foster child, twenty-month-old Bobby, who was found wandering around town alone in a snowstorm, abandoned by his drug-addicted mother.

All three boys are affectionately involved with Bobby, who is perceived as the family pet. Mrs. Carter enjoys the toddler's need for affection, since she considers that her own boys have grown beyond this.

Larry dropped out of school in the eleventh grade. He has not been able to find steady work since. He does not report to his probation officer as regularly as required, but the officer plans to approve Larry's early release from probation so that he can go into the army. Brother James, eighteen, was involved with Larry in the car theft, for which he was sent to the reformatory for 6 months. James is also a school dropout. Despite looking for work for several months since his release, he has been unsuccessful other than odd jobs with Larry and occasional temporary work on construction sites. Their mother feels that association with a group of neighborhood kids who have consistently been involved in criminal activity was the cause of her sons' getting into trouble. Larry and James deny currently seeing these friends, but both their mother and the probation officer believe they are still involved. Youngest brother Kenny, fifteen, has not been in trouble. He earns fair grades in the tenth grade. Mrs. Carter hopes that he will be unlike his brothers and finish school.

The mother is close to a sister who lives nearby. Every day she checks on her elderly father who lives alone. Mrs. Carter is active in her church and the Eastern Star organization, but she does not like people to drop in on her at home and seems to be a shy person. The boys no longer want to accompany her to church, but they relate affectionately to her and work together at trying to fix up their dilapidated housing. All of the boys are required to do regular chores and their own washing and ironing.

Income—consisting of AFDC, the child welfare agency's payment for Bobby's foster care, Mr. Carter's sometime contributions, and what the three boys can make from odd jobs—is nowhere near adequate for the family's needs. Housing is of adequate size, but like the other houses in the neighborhood it is in very poor condition, with window frames pulling away from the walls and the front door literally off its hinges. Nearby houses are in equally poor shape; the neighborhood is a very depressed area, with many burned-out buildings and no care by the city of streets and sidewalks. The area is known for its very high crime rate and is considered unsafe even during the daytime.

The three boys proudly showed the student interviewer the new front porch they had built with the help of an adult friend. Further renovations are planned, as the family's limited budget will allow. The interior of the house is neat, but the furniture is decrepit, looking as if it had been picked up as piecemeal discards.

This black single mother cares about her children and they care about her. She seems to perform well in the parental functions of child nurturance and discipline within the home. But she is not able to control the influences that have an impact on the boys from *outside* the home once they reach adolescence. Several of the other families described here were also in a position of attempting to rear children with respect for prosocial normative values in the face of antagonistic social and neighborhood forces; but the prognosis for them might be considered to be more positive than for the Carter family. This family has the most severe degree of *poverty* of all the families reported in our case vignettes. Other families reported needed to struggle also with racism and poor neighborhood conditions, but housing and neighborhood conditions are not as bad for the other families, and they had a somewhat stronger economic base in terms of the presence of at least one wage-earner who is physically in good enough health to hold down a job consistently (even though that job might be menial and ill-paid). But in the Carter case we have a sick, albeit still young, mother. The physical conditions for the family are substandard; and despite the efforts of the teenage sons, they will never be more than substandard. There is also nothing that the mother can do about this; in fact, the reasonable expectation is that things will get worse, not better.

The positive quality of Mrs. Carter's relationship with

her children, the cleanliness of their dilapidated home, and so on might mean that if adequate financial support had been available for this family earlier, together with adequate community control of neighborhood physical deterioration and crime, Mrs. Carter might have been able to protect her growing boys from delinquency. Given her and the family's environmental situation, however, it is difficult to be optimistic. Larry might make it if he gets away from the neighborhood by going into the army, but it is not realistic to expect with any certainty that he and his brothers will never again be involved in law violation.

There may be pathological forces within this family, but they are not evident from the data of the case as known so far. What role the father plays with his sons, since he does see them weekly, needs to be explored. Why is he unemployed, one wonders—because of a job market that relegates many uneducated black men like him to unemployment? Or additionally, is there perhaps a problem with alcohol or drugs? The nature of the marital relationship between him and Mrs. Carter and the reason for their separation also are not known.

The children observe their parents and their neighbors in this forgotten burned-out slum as having been defeated by the circumstances that surround them. Making a quick buck in whatever way comes to hand is a survival tactic for the people who live in the Carter neighborhood; middleclass normative values militate against, not for, survival. It would take most remarkable parents to oppose successfully the reality of this physical and attitudinal environment. A "good" kid in a "good" family may be destroyed by a sick environment.

A major thrust of intervention in this and several of the other cases reported here would seem to need to be toward efforts to ameliorate that environment. The individual practitioner and agency face a multitude of constraints in attempting to do this for a particular case, since they are operating from a limited power base. The environmental pathology here is not, however, only an individual matter; it applies to all of the Carters trapped in similar circumstances. Intervention therefore needs to consist of translating "private troubles" into "public issues" at a policy level.

Neither individual adolescent, nor family, nor environment can be seen separately since all interdigitate with and affect each other. Each needs to be diagnostically located somewhere on continuua similar to those depicted in Figures 5-1, 5-2 and 5-3.

Problem analysis is not an easy task; it is very difficult and complex. The practitioner is literally snowed under by a blizzard of data, some correlated with others, many that do not seem to be connected, but always with gaps of important data that are simply missing and may never be known. The task is further compounded by the necessity of drawing inferential conclusions from the facts—while remaining clear that inferences are not the same as facts. The analytic process is oriented to answering such questions as "what is the matter," meaning why does the problem exist—what are the causative (if the present development of theory can allow us to know this), contributory, precipitating, and/or exacerbating factors and forces that are involved in the problem's existence? The ultimate purpose of analytic thinking in the case is to answer the question "What needs to be done about the problem—what are the key factors to attempt to change in order to bring about change in the situation?"

The difficulty of this task is such that it is not surprising that the practitioner may tend to leap to premature intellectual closure by attachment to a particular theory. Theory—either that which purports to explain people and the

Figure 5-1. Adolescent Diagnostic Continuum

1	2	3	4	5	6
"Normal" youngster: no marked pathology		Either some intrapsychic pathology that is, however, not clearly associated with the delinquent behavior, and/ or specific defects such as retardation that complicate adolescent's ability to deal with life situation	Intrapsychic pathology causally associated with the delinquent behavior, e.g., rage, need to strike back		Sociopath

Figure 5-2. Family Diagnostic Continuum

1	2	3	4	5	6
"Normal" family		"Normal" family dealing with intrafamily stress, e.g., illness, unemployment	More . . . less functional parenting skills and family structure		Actively psychotic or otherwise severely deficient parents with poor prognosis for intervention; or "criminal" family

Figure 5-3. Environmental Diagnostic Continuum

1	2	3	4	5	6
"Average expectable environment"		Diminishing environmental resources and support: income, housing, community services, neighborhood acceptance, etc.			Hostile, depriving, and/or prodelinquency environment

troubles they get into, such as delinquency, or that which prescribes the intervention to be taken by the practitioner—cannot be used to control or replace the practitioner's own cognitive analytic processes. The practitioner has the responsibility to attempt to "make sense" of the data in the case, at first in as nontheoretical, commonsense a way as possible. The practitioner can turn to theory (or more probably, in most cases to a multiplicity of theories) for illumination of understanding of some of the data in the case or the connections among various sets of data. This implies the necessity of knowing, in some depth, a number of explanatory theories that relate to individual functioning, family functioning, the impact of the environment, and the phenomenon of delinquency; and the necessity of choosing among these in a discriminating fashion those aspects of one or more theories that help the practitioner better to understand relevant aspects of the case.

Intervention, logically and ethically, must follow—not precede—the analysis of the data of the case and must fit that analysis. Intervention might then be perceived as falling somewhere along the same kind of continuua suggested for problem analysis. Intervention continuua are depicted in Figures 5-4, 5-5 and 5-6.

Neither the diagnostic nor the interventive subcategories are, of course, mutually exclusive: a given case might fall anywhere on each of the three diagnostic continuua in Figures 5-1, 5-2 and 5-3, related to the three dimensions of individual, family, and environment. That diagnostic assessment (or problem analysis) will direct whether intervention is needed in any or all of the three dimensions in Figures 5-4, 5-5 and 5-6 and, if so, will provide clues to the kind of intervention called for. Intervention, of course, might well be multiple within as well as across categories, e.g., individual therapy of the youngster *plus* family therapy *plus* intervention with the environment.

Figure 5-4. Adolescent Intervention Continuum

1	2	3	4	5	6
No intervention with adolescent directly; support of parents' handling	Involving parents and adolescent in contracting; possibly also school		Involving parents and adolescent in family therapy aimed at change of family system	Individual (or group) therapy of adolescent	Residential placement of adolescent

Figure 5-5. Family Intervention Continuum

1	2	3	4	5	6
No "therapy": support of parents' present handling and efforts to "de-label" delinquent child	Teaching new parenting skills, contracting, etc.		Family therapy aimed at systemic change of family structure/process	Teaching basic parenting skills, probably also structuring of disorganized family	Possibly removal of child if intervention not effective

Figure 5-6. Environmental Intervention Continuum

1	2	3	4	5	6
Protection of child and family from juvenile justice system and unneeded professional intruders			Securing and coordination of community (material and service) resources		Advocacy and social action re negative environment

201

The Role of the Family

The research evidence is clear that most juvenile delinquents do not go on to adult delinquency. Several factors are undoubtedly involved in this phenomenon, especially the role of maturation. But the evidence of other research indicates that the role played by the family is also critically important (Coull et al., 1982).

It is unfortunate that some helping professionals tend to see only the resources that *they* offer as relevant to the problems referred to them. But the effectiveness of Alcoholics Anonymous and other nonprofessional natural helping systems indicates that naturally existing helping resources are indeed useful to many people. The family represents such a resource. The pathological family has great power to hurt. The ordinary family has great power to heal and to help, and it has more power to do so than any outsider professional. It may need some help from the professional to enable it to recognize and marshal its resources, or it may be able to help its youngster with only support from the professional. With families that do possess this potential (and these are probably the majority of families in at least the less serious forms of adolescent delinquency), the role of the professional becomes that of collaborating with and supporting the family as the primary agency of help for the youngster. The family, not the professional, is in the central position.

Chapter 6

TOWARD A MODEL OF INTERVENTION FOR JUVENILE DELINQUENCY

Resocialization: Goal, Process, Means

The *goal* of resocialization is the modification of the attitudes, skills, or behaviors of the delinquent so that antisocial behavior does not recur.

The *process* by which this aim is achieved involves engagement of the adolescent offender with those persons and societal institutions that possess both (1) the right and (2) the capacity to influence or change his attitudes, skills, or behaviors.

The *means* of resocialization involve the specifics of particular actions by these persons and institutions directed toward the goal of influencing change in the offender's attitudes, skills, and behaviors.

An ultimate model of intervention will need to take into account these three complex variables (and each, in turn, consists of subsets of equally complex subordinate variables).

There is not much controversy concerning the "why," or goal, of resocialization of the delinquent: professionals and the public at large agree on the goal of change of attitudes, skills, or behaviors so that delinquency does not recur. Where controversy does exist is in the definition of the "what," or process of resocialization. Even more controversial is the issue of "who"—who should be involved in the process.

The history of treatment of juvenile delinquency describes a shift over time in the definitions of the "what" and the "who" of resocialization. American society started from a punitive definition: "juvenile delinquents are bad boys and girls who need to be punished to impress on them the error of their ways." In this definition, the process of resocialization was incarceration, and the relevant actors in the process were jailers. Next came a more humanitarian definition: "juvenile delinquents are confused, unloved, but primarily 'sick' kids who need treatment by skilled mental health professionals." In this definition, the process of resocialization was considered to be psychotherapy, and the relevant actors were mental health professionals. Other treatment approaches, such as behavioral programs that emphasize reconditioning of behavior patterns and educational programs that focus on skills training, appear to be variants of these definitions.

All of these approaches point to some successes with some youngsters, but the evidence does not indicate substantial effectiveness on any broad scale with a large variety of the different kinds of adolescents who commit delinquent acts. In general, the definition of the "what" and the "who" of the resocialization process at present seems to consist of administrative—in this instance, meaning bureaucratic—remediation. As has also been the case with the public schools, the problem of delinquency is dumped on probation services primarily, with little involvement or concern on the part of the public; and the response of the bureaucratic structure is to seek out what Tierney (1982) termed "dispositions" of the case. Rather than asking what has happened to this youngster, family, and community that has resulted in delinquency, or what needs to happen differently now, the bureaucratic-dispositional approach asks: "From the packaged dispositions we have available, what can this agency do with this delinquent?" The administrative dispositions that are available include monitoring by the probation officer, referral to a mental health agency, and placement out of the home, either to a treatment-oriented residential program or to a correctional facility.

THE ROLE OF PROBATION OR YOUTH-SERVING AGENCY

Probation operates under a difficult double mandate. It was developed from a humanitarian orientation, with its purpose perceived as that of facilitating the resocialization of the delinquent without recourse to segregating him from family, school, and his normal life context. Delinquents are seen as children in need of help and guidance, not punishment. At the same time, however, the second mandate charges probation with monitoring the behavior of the delinquent toward the goal of protecting the community from further delinquent acts. When the inherently conflictual nature of this dual mandate is added to such other stresses as large caseloads and lack of training of probation officers, the difficulties of the role become manifest.

As serious a problem for the effective dispensation of probation services inheres in the usual societal perception of probation. Probation, not the family, is commonly considered to bear the *primary* responsibility for resocialization of the juvenile offender. This tends to produce two negative effects: the family as a resource is ignored, and the probation officer is forced to assume full responsibility for the resocialization task. In most cases, however, the officer is attempting this task from a position of relative powerlessness. The resources that a probation officer can mobilize to effect resocialization are only three: (1) his authority position and the legal sanctions he can call on in the event of further violations; (2) his personal relationship with the juvenile; and (3) his access to other community services to which he can refer the youth or family.

The threat of legal sanctions, should he violate probation regulations or engage in further delinquency, does serve as a deterrent to some delinquents; but given the insouciance characteristic of adolescence and the inability of probation to monitor every aspect of an adolescent's behavior, there are many delinquents who are not deterred. Some adults refer to the relationship with a probation officer in their youth as the critical experience in their rehabilitation; but many delinquents do not want a relationship with this authority figure, and in any case, the overworked probation officer has time to offer a close relationship to only a few of the youngsters in his large caseload. Additionally, a relationship with the probation officer cannot reasonably be expected to represent a powerful enough single force to substantively change the course of delinquency for many youngsters.* Further, the juvenile's need is for constructive relationships with the most influential and permanent people in his life—his family. Referral to community services and programs is helpful to those youngsters and families who need them, but it is unusual for a probation officer to be able to conduct a sufficiently adequate assessment of adolescent and family in their social context to make an informed judgment as to which community services are needed and for which the

---

*See, for example, the case of Eddie Marciano, pp. 165–168, who did have a close relationship with his accepting and caring probation officer but for whom it is unrealistic to expect that this relationship *alone* will be sufficient help for his multiple and serious problems.

adolescent and/or family are ready. Even when properly assessed needs are appropriately matched with existent community services, the typical probation officer rarely has the time to prepare his clients to use the referrals or to monitor whether the referral actually "took" in terms of the clients becoming productively engaged with the community service. (In our study sample, many needs of individual youngsters and families that appropriately called for some community service had gone unnoticed by probation; and even when referrals had been made, the probation officer had rarely been able to follow up consistently enough to insure that the linkage with the community service had actually taken place.)

Socialization is primarily the task of the family, and the family is the best suited of all societal institutions to carry out this task, by virtue of its emotional investment in the child and the societal expectations of parental roles. This does not mean, of course, that socialization is solely the responsibility of the family. Although few communities have the full quantity or quality of community services that are needed, our social system does offer many kinds of services—educational, religious, health care, recreational—that supplement and support what is also the primary role of the family in these areas as well. It is only when the family proves totally inadequate to fulfill its socialization function that the community must try to provide a substitute in the form of foster home, group home, or institution.

There is no lack of experimentation with new approaches to delinquency, including diversion programs, special programs in police departments, court sentences to perform community service, and so on. Few of these programs provide reliable measures as yet of their effectiveness, and the effectiveness of traditional probation services for juvenile delinquency has never been demonstrated. Our suggestions for an ultimate intervention model do not invariably call for a probation service role, since such a role could conceivably be delegated to youth service agencies working with the police and the courts. However, in the United States probation departments are the most logical arena for experimentation with the development of this model. In the first place, probation services are *there*—i.e., an administrative agency structure with staffing, funding, and an established relationship with police and the courts is in place. Second, the broad mandate of probation, which includes rehabilitation, leaves room for the very functions we are advocating. The observation that *traditional* probation services have never been demonstrated to be particularly effective in dealing with juvenile delinquency does not remove the challenge facing the correctional system and the community at large to develop probation into an effective instrument for dealing with juvenile offenders.

We are proposing that probation services be held accountable for the following four major functions:

1. Problem analysis or psychosocial assessment of the three dimensions of delinquent youngster, family, and social context as outlined earlier. The assessment is oriented toward identifying those factors, in any or all of the three dimensions, that appear to be causative, contributory, perpetuating, or exacerbating of the delinquent behavior. Additionally, the assessment is consciously and deliberately focused on identifying the resources that exist within these three dimensions that can be mobilized to help the youngster move beyond his delinquency to undertake more effectively the normal tasks of adolescent development.

2. Development of a rehabilitation plan that is soundly grounded in the psychosocial assessment, i.e., one that specifies what actions need to be taken, and by whom, to counteract those factors related to the delinquent himself, to his family, and/or to their social context that have been identified as supportive of his delinquent behavior; and that also specifies what actions need to be taken, and

by whom, to mobilize the present or potential resources for rehabilitation that have been identified in each of the three dimensions.

3.   Monitoring of the rehabilitation plan, or "case management." This term is perhaps not the most felicitous one because of its semantic overtones of "managing" or processing people. However, it is the term currently in use to describe a role in which the case manager usually does not undertake direct treatment responsibilities but rather is responsible for seeing to it that what needs to be done in a given case indeed is done—in other words, that the rehabilitation plan is actually carried out (Ryan, 1976; Johnson & Rubin, 1983). Such a rehabilitation plan for one delinquent may be rather simple and parsimonious, but for many others it will be complex and subject to repeated reviews and modifications as further information becomes available, including information about the response of youngster, family, and social context to interventive efforts. With a caseload consisting of some number of the latter types of cases, the job of the case manager can become a full-time one.

4.   The last major function for the probation service is its traditional one of monitoring whether further violations of law or of the court-set terms of probation have occurred, so as to provide some (albeit realistically minimal) protective insurance to the community.

IMPLEMENTATION OF PROBATION FUNCTIONS

Execution of the problem analysis and construction of the rehabilitation plan based on it is a professional task. It needs to be carried out by persons with graduate-level training in a mental health discipline, preferably social work, which is more oriented than the other mental health professions to the concept of person-*in-situation*.

The third and fourth functions can well be carried out by regular probation officers. A high probability exists, however, that unless some effective linkage is structured between the mental health professional and the probation officers, the carefully worked-out assessment and rehabilitation plan of the professional will be disregarded or somehow lost in the shuffle at the point at which probation officers must implement it. This is too frequently the fate of such diagnostic evaluations and treatment recommendations commonly provided by specialized diagnostic clinics to referring public agencies such as probation, public welfare, and child welfare. Additionally, such outside specialized agencies rarely have enough knowledge of the kinds of reality constraints and pressures on the personnel of the referring public agencies and of the unavailability of resources in the particular community that render impracticable the full implementation of the specialists' idealized treatment recommendations.

It would therefore seem important that the mental health professional responsible for the assessment and plan of resocialization be an employed staff member of the probation department. Increasingly, probation services are employing such professionals. In the geographic area where the authors are located these professionals are most frequently used to deliver directly some highly specialized treatment modality: In one local probation department a professional does psychoanalytically oriented psychotherapy with a small caseload of adolescents (the family is never seen); in another, a psychologist conducts family therapy with an equally small and selected caseload. In the authors' judgment this is not the best use of trained mental health professionals in the probation context. For one thing, it is duplicatory of such services already available in other community agencies such as mental health centers and is therefore not cost-effective. Further, it is the authors' observation that morale of probation officers is impaired by what they perceive as the status difference between themselves and the minority professional "elite" whom they perceive as having a much easier job in terms of their comparatively tiny caseloads. Finally, and perhaps most important, direct delivery of various "therapies" is not the task of probation. There is no way that enough trained professionals can be employed, or enough probation officers with bachelor's degrees can receive graduate mental health training, to deliver individual and/or family therapies to all who need them in the very large caseloads with which probation services must deal. Even if this were possible, it would seem to make little sense for a probation department to set out to imitate its neighboring community mental health center or family service agency. Probation is different from such agencies, with a different mandate and therefore different functions to perform.

One possible administrative model for performance of the four major probation functions might well be that developed and empirically tested by Schwartz (1966, 1972) and Schwartz and Sample (1967). In this intervention-research project in a large public welfare agency, one experimental variable was the innovative use of master's-level social workers. Rather than attempting to use these trained practitioners to directly deliver interventive services to clients, an administrative arrangement was set up in which the MSW was responsible for diagnostic assessment of the needs of individual cases and for planning the strategy of intervention related to that assessment. The professional workers headed teams of bachelor's-level personnel who were responsible for carrying out the intervention plan; however, the trained professional retained overall responsibility for the cases *and* for their outcomes. The research findings indicated demonstrated effectiveness for this administrative model, as compared to the usual arrangement in public welfare agencies where, if MSWs are employed at all, they are usually utilized as supervisors of untrained workers, with the latter having responsibility for their own caseloads.

This administrative pattern would seem to hold some promise for application to probation, with a few modifications to adapt it to the probation context. The mental health professional and several regular probation officers might constitute a "team" or "unit" handling either a generic caseload or perhaps a specialized one, e.g., cases from a given community. (In fact, a good rationale could be presented for units each responsible for certain communities or sections of a large community, since it would be imperative for the probation officers to be intimately knowledgeable about the community and its resources and to be on a first-name basis with the staffs of those community programs.) The professional would be responsible for the psychosocial assessment, the development of the rehabilitation plan, and the *outcome* of all of the unit's cases. In some instances the assessment might be based totally on information about youngster, family, and social context developed by the probation officer; in other cases, however, the professional would need to be responsible for developing the data used for assessment him- or herself through home and community visits as well as office contacts, and in some cases the use as well of specialized diagnostic services of other community agencies. Probation officers would be responsible for case management, meaning insuring that all aspects of the rehabilitation plan were actually carried out. This involves negotiating contracts between the delinquent/family and the various actors, professional and informal, who have been identified as being able to offer some resource or service. These might well include, for example, mental health workers in a community agency, school personnel, health care clinics and providers, public welfare and child welfare staff involved with the case, the public housing office, staff of community recreational programs, and so on. The probation officer would be responsible also for keeping the professional unit leader apprised of difficulties encountered in implementing the resocialization plan that necessitate either intervention with the family or with the community helpers involved, or perhaps the need to review and modify the assessment and/or the plan.

Triage Functions

Implicit in the suggestion for how assessment and intervention might be professionally conducted and administratively facilitated is the concept of *triage*, i.e., the sorting out of cases, based on assessment, into three groups:

(1)   those cases in which the professional judgment is that only minimal intervention and time will be required beyond support of the family and possibly referral to recreational and other such community resources;

(2)   those cases in which the judgment is for a good prognosis but where intensive intervention in any or all of the three dimensions will be required;

(3)   those cases in which the prognosis is assessed to be not good, either because the resources available to counteract the negative forces contributing to the adolescent's delinquency are insufficient or because no known interventive technique yet exists to deal with them. The agency has the obligation, of course, to attempt to work with these cases; it may even find itself inventing new interventive approaches as a result of the experience.

The purpose of triage is to deploy time and staff resources as expeditiously and efficiently as possible, to ensure that the agency is not overreaching on some cases that do not need as much time and interventive effort at the expense of other cases that do need this but are thereby shortchanged. Probation officers now do conduct a kind

of triage operation on their caseloads but in an unsystematic and idiosyncratic way. The use of professional assessment as a guide to triage decisions should render the
service not only of higher quality and more focused in
purpose but also more cost-effective.

The role of the family in the resocialization process
needs to be highlighted in both the assessment and the
rehabilitation plan. The salient role of the family in the
etiology as well as the treatment of delinquency does not,
of course, guarantee a constructive family role in the resocialization of the young offender. The limited analysis
presented in Chapter 3 as applied to two samples suggests,
however, that *most* families are in a position to contribute
to this process. The nature of the contribution will vary
widely depending on family strengths and motivations. A
minimal contribution may take the form of some obvious
interest in the welfare of their delinquent offspring and
passive cooperation with the rehabilitation plan. Midrange
will be found many families who will welcome and will utilize help from a community agency to which they are referred for their internal family problems that are either
playing some role in the youngster's need to act out or that
are preventing the family from assuming its socialization
function. Such families will be likely to cooperate actively
with other components of the resocialization plan. At the
most positive pole will be well-functioning families who are
capable of assuming a full supervisory and guidance role
for their adolescent and who will work closely with community resources identified in the resocialization plan as
having some helpful part to play. And, of course, there
will be some families where the initial assessment and/or
the family's ensuing demonstrated inability to respond to
intervention indicate that they cannot play a constructive
role in resocialization of the youth and that other plans
for the youngster are necessary.

A hardly unimportant consideration is that of the costs

of a program such as we have outlined here. At a time like the present, when service cost containment is politically one of the most sensitive issues, the chances of mounting a new and costly program, no matter how promising, are small indeed. Although the ultimate evaluation of cost would require demonstration studies in a variety of settings, the basic design of the kind of program we have suggested should not require a more costly operation than that called for by traditional juvenile probation settings. There would be, to be sure, some anticipated increase in expenditure for the employment of master's-level professionals as unit leaders responsible for comprehensive assessments and planning of resocialization strategy. As noted earlier, however, many probation departments are at present employing such professionals (although we have taken issue with the way in which they are currently used). The cost of employing professionals in the way we have proposed might well be counterbalanced by the delegation of resocialization functions away from the probation officer to families, and to community resources that are at present often not sufficiently utilized.

The family is unquestionably the *most* underutilized resource in the corrections field, despite the fact that it has the greatest investment in the well-being of its young. The predominant service pattern of, at best, leaving the initiative for involvement up to the parents, or, at worst, keeping the family entirely isolated from treatment, has done little to encourage family participation or to harness and mobilize its potential for resocialization of the offender.

The Family or Juvenile Court

Existing family court laws by and large lack mechanisms for a reliable assessment of the often complex family circumstances that are encountered in situations of delinquent youth. Our proposal suggests such a mechanism. In the absence of an assessment that takes full account of the individual, the family, and the social context, family-focused rehabilitative efforts are likely to constitute no more than continuing excursions into somebody's favorite therapeutic enclave and/or destructively coercive pressure on already stressed families rather than the help they need.

A number of states in recent years have passed legislation encouraging or mandating family involvement in dealing with juvenile delinquency. Our proposal is not antithetical; in fact, it should serve to implement and insure family involvement because of its focus on the family as a resource to be respected and utilized. We have discussed how the approach might be employed within a probation service; but the team or unit of professional team leader plus a number of case managers could also be integrated into a variety of other legal and organizational arrangements. For example, in some regions where the probation service is poor in quality or is politicized, it may be more feasible to establish this administrative arrangement in a private youth-serving agency with specially drawn linkages to the juvenile or family court.

A Model for a Model

The full dynamic of a model of intervention in juvenile delinquency that offers comprehensive assessment and re-socialization planning, with organizational arrangements that support this approach, calls for model building based on more extensive field research than we were able to accomplish in this beginning study. By design, our effort did not aspire to the goal of development of a fully conceptualized and fully tested model of intervention. We have presented what can best be termed a model for a model. Its value, we believe, lies in the fact that it has not been developed according to the usual nonempirical, theoretical pattern but rather out of our own case analyses and a careful review of the relevant research of others.

Although we do not attempt to present a fully developed model, we do suggest that that ultimate model should possess the following essential characteristics.

1. Emphasis should be placed on comprehensive and sophisticated problem analysis or assessment as to the meaning of the delinquent act from within the perspective of the young offender as a unique individual, in the context of his or her family, and both youngster and family within the wider context of their social reality.

2. The model should require that the resocialization plan be grounded in and justified by the assessment. The data of the case, not some interventive theory or technique *in vacuuo,* should guide the differential choice of particular interventive activities. The rehabilitation plan should be clearly and sharply targeted at specific factors to be supported or to be changed (and it must justify why the latter are considered changeable given the resources available).

3. The model should require that the assessment highlight whether, to what extent, and in what specific ways the family can play a role in the resocialization process. Since the great majority of families can do this, with support, the rehabilitation plan should specifically respect the role of the family as a "natural mental health agency" for its youngster; i.e., the plan should not call for professional intrusions into functions that the family can carry out better.

4. In those cases in which the psychosocial assessment calls for intervention beyond only support of the family's resocialization function, the model should provide for a differential—and probably multiple—selection from a broad range of interventions targeted toward individual, family, and/or the social environment.

5. Evaluation of outcome in individual cases, as well

as cases in the aggregate, needs to be an integral feature of the model. This will require the professional to think out, *in advance* of implementing the intervention plan decided on, the answers to the questions: "What will the youngster, the family, and social context have to look like for me to call this case a success? What specific factors will have to have changed, and what will be observable, valid, and reliable indicators of those changes? Is it reasonable and feasible, given the data of the case and the resources available, to 'shoot for' an ideal goal, or should the goals be limited to partial change, or perhaps only to prevention of further deterioration?"

6. Finally, the model will have to include agency administrative arrangements that make it possible for the model to be actually carried out in practice.

We hope that our "model for a model" represents a convincing rationale supporting the promise of a new direction for resocializing juvenile delinquents, and that it will give rise to an operational model that can be field-tested by means of rigorous research procedure. The final verdict on the worth of our work awaits a successful validation and cross-validation of the ultimate model against the background of an expanding knowledge base about the characteristics of juvenile delinquents, their families, and their social contexts.

REFERENCES

Aichhorn, A. (1935). *Wayward youth*. New York: Viking Press.

Akers, R. L., Krohn, M. D., Lanza-Kaduce, L., & Radosevich, M. (1979). Social learning and deviant behavior: A specific test of a general theory. *American Sociological Review, 44,* 636–655.

Alexander, J. F., & Barton, C. (1976). Behavioral systems therapy with delinquent families. In Olson, D. (Ed.), *Treating relationships*. Lake Mills, IA: Graphic Publishers.

Alexander, J. F., Barton, C., Schiavo, R. S., & Parsons, B. V. (1976). Systems-behavioral intervention with families of delinquents: Therapist characteristics, family behavior, and outcome. *Journal of Consulting and Clinical Psychology, 44,* 656–664.

Alexander, J. F., & Parsons, B. V. (1973). Short-term behavioral intervention with delinquent families: Impact on family process and recidivism. *Journal of Abnormal Psychology, 81,* 219–225.

Alexander, J. F., & Parsons, B. V. (1982). *Functional family therapy.* Monterey, CA: Brooks Cole.

Alfaro, J. D. (1978). *Summary report on the relationship between child abuse and neglect, and later socially deviant behavior.* Unpublished manuscript.

Alvord, J. R. (1971). The home token economy: A motivational system for the home. *Corrective Psychiatry and Journal of Social Therapy, 17,* 6–13.

Andrew, J. M. (1976). Delinquency, sex, and family variables. *Social Biology, 23,* 168–171.

Andry, R. G. (1962). Parental affection and delinquency. In Wolfgang, M. E., Savitz, L., & Johnston, N. (Eds.), *The sociology of crime and delinquency* pp. 330–352. New York: John Wiley.

Andry, R. G. (1971). *Delinquency and parental pathology.* London: Staples Press.

Bahr, S. J. (1979). Family determinants and effects of deviance. In Burr, W. R., Hill, R., Nye, F. I., and Reiss, I. L. (Eds.), *Contemporary theories about the family* pp. 615–643. New York: The Free Press.

Bandura, A., & Walters, R. H. (1959). *Adolescent aggression.* New York: Ronald Press.

Baron, R., & Feeney, F. (1976). *Juvenile diversion through family counseling.* Washington, DC: Law Enforcement Assistance Administration, U.S. Department of Justice.

Beal, D. & Duckro, P. (1977). Family counseling as an alternative to legal action for the juvenile status offender. *Journal of Marriage and Family Counseling, 3,* 77–81.

Becker, H. S. (1963). *Outsiders.* New York: The Free Press.

Berleman, W., Seaberg, J., & Steinburn, T. (1972). The delinquency prevention experiment of the Seattle Atlantic Street Center: A final evaluation. *Social Service Review, 46,* 323–346.

Biles, D. (1971). Birth order and delinquency. *Australian Psychologist, 6,* 189–193.

Birchler, G., and Spinks, S. (1980). Behavioral-systems marital and family therapy: Integration and clinical application. *American Journal of Family Therapy, 8,* 6–28.

Bowlby, J. (1952). *Maternal care and mental health*. Geneva: World Health Organization.

Bowlby, J., Ainsworth, M., Boston, M., & Rosenbluth, D. (1956). The effects of mother-child separation: A follow-up study. *British Journal of Medical Psychology, 29,* 211–247.

Brim, O. G. (1966). Socialization through the life cycle. In Brim, Orville G., and Wheeler, Stanton (Eds.), *Socialization after childhood* pp. 3–49. New York: John Wiley and Sons.

Brodkin, A. M. (1980). Family therapy: The making of a mental health movement. *American Journal of Orthopsychiatry, 50,* 4–17.

Byles, J. S., and Maurice, A. (1979). The juvenile services project: An experiment in delinquency control. *Canadian Journal of Criminology, 21,* 155–165.

Carr, A., Gelles, R. J., & Hargreaves, E. F. (1978). *Family composition and its relation to child maltreatment and juvenile delinquency.* Unpublished manuscript.

Carr-Saunders, A. M., Mannheim, H., & Rhodes, E. C. (1942). *Young offenders.* Cambridge: Cambridge University Press.

Chilton, R. J., & Markle, G. E. (1972). Family disruption, delinquent conduct and the effect of sub-classification. *American Sociological Review, 37,* 93–99.

Clausen, J. A. (1968). Perspectives on childhood socialization. In Clausen, J. A. (Ed.), *Socialization and society* pp. 130–181. Boston: Little Brown.

Coalition of Family Organizations. (1979). *COFO memo: A publication of the coalition of family organizations, 2.*

Cohen, A. K. (1955). *Delinquent boys: The culture of the gang.* Glencoe, IL: The Free Press.

Congalton, A. A. (1969). *Status and prestige in Australia.* Melbourne: F. W. Cheshire.

Coughlin, F., & Wimberger, H. C. (1968). Group family therapy. *Family Process, 7,* 37–50.

Coull, V. C. (1978). *The role of the family in the resocialization of juvenile offenders.* Unpublished master's thesis, University of Melbourne.

Coull, V. C., Geismar, L. L. & Waff, A. (1982). The role of family in the resocialization of juvenile offenders. *Journal of Comparative Family Studies, 13*, 63–75.

Craig, M. M., & Furst, P. W. (1965). What happens after treatment? A study of potentially delinquent boys. *Social Service Review, 39*, 165–171.

Craig, M. M., & Glick, S. J. (1963). *Crime and delinquency.* New York: New York City Youth Board.

Cutter, A. V., & Hallowitz, D. (1962). Diagnosis and treatment of the family unit with respect to the character-disordered youngster. *Journal of the American Academy of Child Psychiatry, 1*, 605–618.

Davidson, W., & Seidman, E. (1974). Studies of behavior modification and juvenile delinquency: A review, methodological critique, and social perspective. *Psychological Bulletin, 81*, 998–1011.

Deitz, G. E. (1969). A comparison of delinquents with nondelinquents on self-concept, self acceptance, and parental identification. *Journal of Genetic Psychology, 115*, 285–295.

Dentler, R. A., & Monroe, L. J. (1961). Social correlates of early adolescent theft. *American Sociological Review, 26*, 733–743.

Donner, J. & Gamson, A. (1968). Experience with multi-family, time-limited, outpatient groups at a community psychiatric clinic. *Psychiatry, 31*, 126–137.

Douds, A., Engelsgjerd, M., & Collingwood, T. (1977). Behavior contracting with youthful offenders and their parents. *Child Welfare, 56*, 409–417.

Druckman, J. M. (1979). A family-oriented policy and treatment program for female juvenile status offenders. *Journal of Marriage and the Family, 41*, 627–636.

Duncan, D. F. (1978). Attitudes toward parents and delinquency in suburban adolescent males. *Adolescence, 13*, 365–369.

Duncan, P. (1968). *Family interaction in parents of neurotic and social delinquent girls.* Unpublished Ph.D. dissertation, University of Wisconsin.

Durkheim, E. (1961). *Moral education*. E. K. Wilson & H. Schnurer, (Trans.). New York: The Free Press.

Eissler, R. S. (1949). Scapegoats of society. In Eissler, K. R. (Ed.), *Searchlights on delinquency* pp. 288–305. New York: International Universities Press.

Ensminger, M. E., Kellam, S. G., & Rubin, B. R. (1983). School and family origins of delinquency: Comparison by sex. In Van Dusen, K. T., & Mednick, S. A. (Eds.), *Prospective studies of crime and delinquency* pp. 73–97. Boston: Kluwer-Nijhoff.

Evans, H. A., Chagoya, L., & Rakoff, V. (1971). Decision-making as to the choice of family therapy in an adolescent inpatient setting. *Family Process, 10,* 97–110.

Famiglietti, J. F. (1981). *Family-strengthening programs, delinquency prevention, and program evaluation: An assessment of efficacy and utilization.* Unpublished Ph.D. dissertation, University of Washington.

Farrington, D. P., Gundry, G., & West, D. J. (1975). The familial transmission of criminality. *Medicine, Science, and the Law, 15,* 177–186.

Feather, N. T., & Cross, D. G. (1975). Value systems and delinquency: Parental and generational discrepancies in value systems for delinquent and non-delinquent boys. *The British Journal of Social and Clinical Psychology, 14,* 117–129.

Feldman, R. A., Caplinger, T. E., & Wodarsky, J. S. (1983). *The St. Louis conundrum. The effective treatment of antisocial youths.* Englewood Cliffs, NJ: Prentice-Hall.

Ferguson, T. (1952). *The young delinquent in his social setting.* Oxford: Oxford University Press.

Ferreira, A. J., & Winter, W. D. (1966). Stability of interactional variables in family decision-making. *Archives of General Psychiatry, 14,* 352–355.

Ferreira, A. J., & Winter, W. D. (1968). Information exchange and silence in normal and abnormal families. *Family Process, 7,* 251–276.

Friedlander, K. (1947). *The psychoanalytic approach to juvenile delinquency.* New York: International Universities Press.

Gable, R. J., & Brown, W. K. (1978). Positive outcomes: A new approach to delinquency research. *Juvenile and Family Court Journal*, 57–64.

Garcia-Preto, N. (1982). Puerto Rican families. In McGoldrick, M., Pearce, J. K., and Giordano, J. (Eds.). *Ethnicity and family therapy* pp. 164–186. New York: Guilford Press.

Garrigan, J. J., & Bambrick, A. (1975). Short-term family therapy with emotionally disturbed children. *Journal of Marriage and Family Counseling, 1*, 379–385.

Garrigan, J. J. & Bambrick, A. (1977). Family therapy for disturbed children: Some experimental results in special education. *Journal of Marriage and Family Counseling, 3*, 83–93.

Geismar, L. L. (1973). *555 families. A social psychological study of young families in transition.* New Brunswick, NJ: Transaction Books.

Geismar, L. L. (1980). *Family and community functioning* (2nd rev. & exp. ed.). Metuchen, NJ: The Scarecrow Press.

Geismar, L. L., & La Sorte, M. A. (1964). *Understanding the multi-problem family.* New York: Association Press.

Geismar, L. L., La Sorte, M. A., & Ayres, B. Measuring family disorganization. *Marriage and Family Living, 24*, 51–56.

Gibb, J. R. (1961). Defensive communications. *Journal of Communications, 3*, 141–148.

Ginsberg, B. G. (1977). Parent-child relationship development program. In Guerney, B. G. (Ed.), *Relationship enhancement* pp. 227–267. San Francisco: Jossey-Bass.

Gluck, M. R., Tanner, M. M., Sullivan, D. F., and Erickson, P. A. (1964). Follow-up evaluation of fifty-five child guidance cases. *Behavioral Research and Therapy, 2*, 131–134.

Glueck, S., & Glueck, E. (1950). *Unraveling juvenile delinquency.* Cambridge, MA: Harvard University Press.

Glueck, S., & Glueck, E. (1957). Working mothers and delinquency. *Mental Hygiene, 41*, 327–352.

Glueck, S., & Glueck, E. (1962). *Family environment and delinquency.* London: Routledge and Kegan Paul.

Glueck, S., & Glueck, E. (1968). *Delinquents and nondelinquents in perspective.* Cambridge, MA: Harvard University Press.

Gold, M. (1963). *Status forces in delinquent boys.* Ann Arbor, MI: Institute for Social Research, University of Michigan.

Grogan, H. J., & Grogan, R. C. (1968). The criminogenic family: Does chronic tension cause delinquency? *Crime and Delinquency, 14,* 220–225.

Gurman, A. S., & Kniskern, D. P. (1978). Research in marital and family therapy: Progress, perspective and prospect. In Garfield, S. L., & Bergin, A. E. (Eds.) *Handbook of psychotherapy and behavior change: An empirical analysis* (2nd ed.). New York: John Wiley.

Haley, J. (1964). Research on family patterns: An instrument measurement. *Family Process, 3,* 41–65.

Haley, J. (1976). *Problem solving therapy.* San Francisco: Jossey-Bass.

Haley, J. (1980). *Leaving home: The therapy of disturbed young people.* New York: McGraw-Hill.

Haskell, M. R. & Yablonsky, L. (1974). *Juvenile delinquency.* Chicago: Rand McNally.

Healy, W., & Bronner, A. (1936). *New light on delinquency and its treatment.* New Haven, CT: Yale University Press.

Hennessy, M., Richards, P. J., & Berk, R. A. (1978). Broken homes and middle class delinquency. *Criminology, 15,* 505–528.

Hirschi, T. (1971). *Causes of delinquency.* Berkeley, CA: University of California Press.

Hutchings, B., and Mednick, S. A. (1974). Registered criminality in the adoptive and biological parents of registered male criminal adoptees. In Fieve, R. R., & Zubin, D. A. (Eds.), *Genetics and psychopathology.* Baltimore: Johns Hopkins Press.

Illich, I. D. (1976). *Medical nemesis: The expropriation of health.* New York: Pantheon Books.

Jacob, T. (1975). Family interaction in disturbed and normal families: A methodological and substantive review. *Psychological Bulletin, 82,* 33–65.

Jaffe, L. (1969). Family anomie and delinquency: Development of the concept and some empirical findings. *British Journal of Criminology, 9,* 376–388.

Jayaratne, S. (1978). Behavioral intervention and family decision-making. *Social Work, 23,* 20–25.

Jayaratne, S., Stuart, R., & Tripodi, T. (1974). Methodological issues and problems in evaluating treatment outcomes in the family and school consultation project. In Davidson, P., Clark, F., & Hamerlynck, L. (Eds.), *Evaluation of behavioral programs in community, residential, and school settings.* Champaign, IL: Research Press.

Jenkins, R. L. (1974). Deprivation of parental care as a contribution to juvenile delinquency. In Robert, A. R. (Ed.), *Childhood deprivation.* Springfield, IL: Charles C. Thomas.

Johnson, A. M. (1949). Sanctions for superego lacunae of adolescents. In Eissler, K. R. (Ed.), *Searchlights on delinquency* pp. 225–246. New York: International Universities Press.

Johnson, P. J., & Rubin, A. (1983). Case management in mental health: A social work domain? *Social Work, 28,* 49–55.

Johnson, R. E. (1979). *Juvenile delinquency and its origins.* Cambridge: Cambridge University Press.

Johnstone, J. W. (1978). Juvenile delinquency and the family: A contextual interpretation. *Youth and Society, 9,* 299–313.

Kaffman, M. (1963). Short-term family therapy. *Family Process, 2,* 216–234.

Kemp, C. J. (1971). Family treatment within the milieu of a residential treatment center. *Child Welfare, 50,* 229–235.

Kennedy, D. B., & Kerber, A. (1973). *Resocialization: An American experiment.* New York: Behavioral Publications.

Kifer, R. E., Lewis, M. A., Green, D. R., & Phillips, E. L. (1974). Training predelinquent youth and their parents to negotiate conflict situations. *Journal of Applied Behavioral Analysis, 7,* 357–364.

Klees, P. S. (1979). *Modifying defensive and supportive communication in families of delinquents.* Unpublished Ph.D. dissertation, Brigham Young University.

Klein, N., Alexander, J. F., & Parsons, B. V. (1977). Impact of family systems intervention on recidivism and sibling delinquency: A model of primary prevention and program evaluation. *Journal of Consulting and Clinical Psychology, 45,* 469–474.

Kraus, J., & Smith, J. (1973). The relationship of four types of "broken home" to some neglected parameters of juvenile delinquency. *Australian Journal of Social Issues, 8,* 52–57.

Krisberg, B., & Austin, J. (1978). *The children of Ishmael.* Palo Alto, CA: Mayfield.

Lane, T. W., & Burchard, J. D. (1983). Failure to modify delinquent behavior: A constructive analysis. In Foa, E. B., & Emmelkamp. P. M. (Eds.), *Failures in behavior therapy* pp. 355–377. New York: John Wiley.

Langner, T. S., McCarthy, E. D., Gersten, J. C., Simcha-Fagan, O., & Eisenberg, J. G. (1979). Factors in children's behavior and mental health over time: The family research project. *Research in Community Mental Health, 1,* 127–181.

Lasch, C. (1977). *Haven in a heartless world: The family besieged.* New York: Basic Books.

Lees, J. P., & Newsom, L. J. (1954). Family or sibling position as some aspects of juvenile delinquency. *British Journal of Delinquency, 5,* 46–65.

Lerman, P. (1970). Evaluative studies of institutions for delinquents. In Lerman, P. (Ed.), *Delinquency and social policy* pp. 317–328. New York: Praeger.

Levitt, E. (1957). The results of psychotherapy with children: An evaluation. *Journal of Consulting Psychology, 21,* 189–196.

Little, V. L., & Kendall, P. C. (1979). Cognitive-behavioral interventions with delinquents: Problem-solving, role-taking, and self-control. In Kendall, P. C., & Hollon, S. D. (Eds.), *Cognitive-behavioral interventions: Theory, research, and procedures* pp. 81–115. New York: Academic Press.

Maccoby, E. E. (1958). Children and working mothers. *The Child, 5,* 83–89.

Maccoby, E. E. (1968). The development of moral values and behavior in childhood. In Clausen, J. A. (Ed.), *Socialization and society* pp. 227–269. Boston: Little Brown.

MacGregor, R. (1962). Multiple impact psychotherapy with families. *Family Process, 1,* 15–29.

MacGregor, R., Ritchie, A. M., Serrano, A. C., Schuster, F. P., McDanald, E. C., & Goolishian, H. A. (1964). *Multiple impact therapy with families.* New York: McGraw-Hill.

Maskin, M. B. (1976). The differential impact of work-oriented versus communication-oriented juvenile correction programs upon recidivism rates in delinquent males. *Journal of Clinical Psychology, 32,* 432–433.

Maskin, M. B., & Brookins, E. (1974). The effects of parental composition on recidivism rates in delinquent girls. *Journal of Clinical Psychology, 30,* 341–342.

Mathews, J. (1923). A survey of 341 delinquent girls in California. *Journal of Delinquency, 8,* 196–231.

McCord, J. (1979). *Consideration of the impact of paternal behavior on subsequent criminality.* Unpublished manuscript.

McCord, J., & McCord, W. (1964). The effects of parental role model on criminality. In Cavan, R. S. (Ed.), *Readings in juvenile delinquency* pp. 170–180. Philadelphia: J. B. Lippincott.

McCord, W., McCord, J., & Zola, I. (1959). *Origins of crime.* New York: Columbia University Press.

McGoldrick, M. (1982). Irish families. In McGoldrick, M., Pearce, J. K., & Giordano, J. (Eds.), *Ethnicity and family therapy* pp. 310–339. New York: Guilford Press.

Menne, J., & Williams, L. (1976). *Iowa research in family therapy with families of delinquent youth.* Des Moines, IA: Iowa Department of Social Services, Family Services Department. (No. 1, March 1974–March 1975; No. 2, April 1975–January 1976; No. 3, February 1976–July 1976.)

Merton, R. K. (1949). Social theory and social structure. In Merton, R. K. (Ed.), *Social structure and anomie* pp. 125–149. Glencoe, IL: The Free Press.

Michaels, K. W., & Green, R. H. (1979). A child welfare agency project: Therapy for families of status offenders. *Child Welfare, 58,* 216–220.

Miller, P. Y., & Simon, W. (1974). Adolescent sexual behavior: Context and change. *Social Problems, 22,* 58–76.

Minuchin, S. (1974). *Families and family therapy.* Cambridge, MA: Harvard University Press.

Minuchin, S., Montalvo, B., Guerney, B., Rosman, B., & Schumer, F. (1967). *Families of the slums.* New York: Basic Books.

Mischler, E., & Waxler, N. (1968). *Interaction in families.* New York: John Wiley.

Monahan, T. (1957). Family status and the delinquent child: A reappraisal of some new findings. *Social Forces, 35,* 250–258.

Norland, S., Shover, N., Thornton, W., & James, J. (1979). Intrafamily conflict and delinquency. *Pacific Sociological Review, 22,* 223–240.

Nye, F. I. (1973). *Family relationships and delinquent behavior.* New York: Wiley, 1958. Westport, CT: Greenwood Press.

Otterstrom, E. (1946). Delinquency and children from bad homes. *Sita Paediatrica, 33* (Suppl. 5).

Parsons, B. V., & Alexander, J. F. (1973). Short-term family intervention: A therapy outcome study. *Journal of Consulting and Clinical Psychology, 41,* 195–201.

Patterson, G. (1974). Interventions for boys with conduct problems: Multiple settings, treatments and criteria. *Journal of Consulting and Clinical Psychology, 42,* 471–481.

Patterson, G. (1978). *Application to the Department of Health, Education and Welfare for funding a research project.* (Privileged communication).

Patterson, G. & Brodsky, G. (1966). A behaviour modification programme for a child with multiple problem behaviours. *Journal of Child Psychology and Psychiatry, 7,* 277–295.

Patterson, G., Cobb, J., & Ray, R. (1973). A social engineering technology for retraining the families of aggressive boys. In Adams, H. E., & Unikel, I. P., (Eds.), *Issues and trends in be-*

havior therapy pp. 139–210. Springfield, IL: Charles C. Thomas.

Patterson, G., McNeal, S., Hawkins, N., & Phelps, R. (1967). Reprogramming the social environment. *Journal of Child Psychology and Psychiatry, 8,* 181–195.

Patterson, G., Ray, R., & Shaw, D. (1968). Direct intervention in families of deviant children. *Oregon Research Institute Bulletin 8,* No. 9.

Patterson, G., & Reid, J. (1973). Intervention for families of aggressive boys: A replication study. *Behavior Research and Therapy, 11,* 383–394.

Platt, A. M. (1977). *The child savers.* Chicago: University of Chicago Press.

Popper, K. (1972). *Conjectures and refutations* (4th ed.). London: Routledge & Kegan Paul.

Postner, R. S., Guttman, H. A., Sigal, J. J., Epstein, N. B., and Rakoff, V. M. (1971). Process and outcome in conjoint family therapy. *Family Process, 10,* 451–473.

Powers, E. & Witmer, H. (1951). *An experiment in the prevention of delinquency: The Cambridge-Somerville Youth Study.* New York: Columbia University Press.

President's Commission on Law Enforcement and Administration of Justice (1967). *Task force report: Juvenile delinquency and youth crime.* Washington, DC: U.S. Government Printing Office.

Rahav, G. (1976). Family relations and delinquency in Israel. *Criminology, 14,* 259–269.

Reid, J. B., & Hendricks, A. (1973). Preliminary analysis of the effectiveness of direct home intervention for the treatment of predelinquent boys who steal. In Hamerlynck, L. A., Handy, L. C., & Mash, E. J. (Eds.), *Behavior change: Methodology, concepts and practice* pp. 209–219. Champaign, IL: Research Press.

Reiss, A. J. (1952). Social correlates of psychological types of delinquency. *American Sociological Review, 17,* 710–780.

Riege, M. G. (1972). Parental affection and juvenile delinquency in girls. *The British Journal of Criminology, 12,* 55–73.

Robin, A. L. (1979). Problem-solving communication training: A behavioral approach to the treatment of parent-adolescent conflict. *American Journal of Family Therapy, 7,* 69–82.

Robin, A. L. (1981). A controlled evaluation of problem-solving communication training with parent-adolescent conflict. *Behavior Therapy, 12,* 593–609.

Robin, A. L. (1983). Parent-adolescent conflict: A developmental problem of families. *Proceedings of the Fifteenth Banff International Conference on Behavior Science.* Banff, Alberta, Canada.

Robin, A. L., Kent, R., O'Leary, K. D., Foster, S., & Prinz, R. (1977). An approach to teaching parents and adolescents problem-solving communication skills: A preliminary report. *Behavior Therapy, 8,* 639–643.

Robins, L. N. (1966). Assessing the contributions of family structure, class and peer groups to juvenile delinquency. *Journal of Criminal Law, Criminology and Police Science, 57,* 325–355.

Robins, L. N. (1966). *Deviant children grown up.* Baltimore: Williams & Wilkins.

Robins, L. N. (1978). Sturdy childhood predictors of adult antisocial behavior: Replication from longitudinal studies. *Psychological Medicine, 8,* 611–622.

Robins, L. N., West, P. A., & Herjanic, B. L. (1975). Arrests and delinquency in two generations: A study of black urban families and their children. *Journal of Child Psychology, 16,* 125–140.

Robison, S. M. (1960). *Juvenile delinquency: Its nature and control.* New York: Henry Holt.

Rodman, H., & Grams, P. (1967). Juvenile delinquency and the family: A review and discussion. In President's Commission on Law Enforcement and Administration of Justice (Eds.), *Task force report: Juvenile delinquency and youth crime.* Washington, DC: Government Printing Office.

Rothman, D. (1978). The state as parent: Social policy in the progressive era. In Gaylin, W., Glasser, I., Marens, S., & Rothman, D. (Eds.), *Doing good: The limits of benevolence*. New York: Pantheon Books.

Rutter, M., & Madge, N. (1976). *Cycles of disadvantage: A review of research*. London: Heineman.

Ryan, R. (1976). Case manager function in the delivery of social services. In Ross, B., & Khinduka, S. K. (Eds.), *Social work in practice* pp. 229–240. Washington, DC: National Association of Social Workers.

Safer, D. J. (1966). Family therapy for children with behavior disorders. *Family Process, 5,* 243–255.

Satir, V. (1964). *Conjoint family therapy*. Palo Alto: Science and Behavior Books.

Schoenberg, R. J. (1975). *A structural model of delinquency*. Unpublished doctoral dissertation, University of Washington.

Schreiber, L. (1966). Evaluation of family group treatment in a family agency. *Family Process, 5,* 21–29.

Schur, E. M. (1971). *Labeling deviant behavior*. New York: Harper and Row.

Schur, E. M. (1973). *Radical non-intervention*. Englewood Cliffs, NJ: Prentice Hall.

Schwartz, E. E. (1966). Strategies of research in public welfare administration: The field experiment. In *Trends in social work practice and knowledge* pp. 164–178. New York: National Association of Social Workers.

Schwartz, E. E. (1972). *The midway office*. New York: National Association of Social Workers.

Schwartz, E. E., & Sample, W. C. (1967). First findings from midway. *Social Service Review, 41,* 113–151.

Shaw, C. R., & McKay, H. D. (1931). Social factors in juvenile delinquency. In *Report on the Causes of Crime* pp. 261–263. Washington, DC: National Commission on Law Observance and Enforcement.

Shaw, C. R., & McKay, H. D. (1932). Are broken homes a causative factor in juvenile delinquency? *Social Forces, 10,* 514–524.

Shaw, R., Blumenfeld, H., & Senf, R. (1968). A short-term treatment program in a child guidance clinic. *Social Work, 13,* 81–90.

Shostak, D. (1977). *Family versus individual-oriented behavior therapy as treatment approaches to juvenile delinquency.* Unpublished doctoral dissertation, University of Virginia.

Shulman, H. M. (1949). The family and juvenile delinquency. *The Annals, American Academy of Political and Social Sciences, 261,* 21–31.

Sigal, J. J., Barrs, C. B., & Doubilet, A. L. (1976). Problems in measuring the success of family therapy in a common clinical setting: Impasse and solutions. *Family Process, 15,* 225–233.

Sigal, J. J., Rakoff, V., & Epstein, N. B. (1967). Indicators of therapeutic outcome in conjoint family therapy. *Family Process, 6,* 215–226.

Slocum, W. L., & Stone, C. L. (1963). Family culture patterns and delinquent-type behavior. *Marriage and Family Living, 25,* 202–208.

Smith, P. M. (1955). Broken homes and juvenile delinquency. *Sociology and Social Research, 39,* 307–311.

Spiegel, D., & Sperber, Z. (1967). Clinical experiment in short-term family therapy. *American Journal of Orthopsychiatry, 37,* 278–279.

Sterne, R. S. (1964). *Delinquent conduct and broken homes.* New Haven, CT: College and University Press.

Stuart, R. (1968). Token reinforcement in marital treatment. In Rubin, R., & Franks, C. (Eds.), *Advances in behavior therapy* pp. 221–230. New York: Academic Press.

Stuart, R. (1971). Behavioral contracting within the families of delinquents. *Journal of Behavior Therapy and Experimental Psychiatry, 2,* 1–11.

Stuart, R., Jayaratne, S., & Tripodi, T. (1976). Changing adolescent deviant behaviour through reprogramming the behaviour of parents and teachers: An experimental evaluation. *Canadian Journal of Behaviour Science, 8,* 132–144.

Stuart, R., & Lott, L. (1972). Behavioral contracting with delinquents: A cautionary note. *Journal of Behavior Therapy and Experimental Psychiatry, 2,* 161–169.

Stuart, R., & Tripodi, T. (1973). Experimental evaluation of three time-constrained behavioral treatments for predelinquents and delinquents. In Rubin, R. R., Brady, J. P., & Henderson, J. D. (Eds.), *Advances in behavior therapy* pp. 1–12. New York: Academic Press.

Stuart, R., Tripodi, T., Jayaratne, S., & Camburn, D. (1976). An experiment in social engineering in serving the families of predelinquents. *Journal of Abnormal Child Psychology, 4,* 243–261.

Stumphauser, J. S. (1970). Behavior modification with juvenile delinquents: A critical review. *Federal Correctional Institute Technical and Treatment Notes, 1,* 1–22.

Sullenger, T. E. (1930). *Social determinants of juvenile delinquency.* Omaha, NE: Douglas.

Sutherland, E. H. (1939). *Principles of criminology.* Chicago: Lippincott.

Sykes, G., & Matza, D. (1957). Techniques of neutralization: A theory of delinquency. *American Sociological Review, 22,* 664–670.

Tait, C., & Hodges, E. (1972). *Delinquents, their families, and the community.* Springfield, IL: Charles C. Thomas.

Tharp, R., & Wetzel, R. (1969). *Behavior modification in the natural environment.* New York: Academic Press.

Tierney, L. (1982). *Submission on children and youth in institutions.* Melbourne, Australia: Melbourne University (mimeographed).

Venezia, P. (1968). Delinquency as a function of intrafamily relationships. *Journal of Research in Crime and Delinquency, 5,* 148–174.

Wahler, R. G., Leske, G., & Rogers, E. S. (1978). *The insular family: A deviance support mechanism for oppositional children.* (Unpublished manuscript).

Walter, H., & Gilmore, S. (1973). Placebo versus social learning effects in parent training procedures designed to alter the behavior of aggressive boys. *Behavior Therapy, 4,* 361–377.

Watson, J. D. (1968). *The double helix.* New York: Atheneum.

Weathers, L., & Liberman, R. (1975). Contingency contracting with families of delinquent adolescents. *Behavior Therapy, 6,* 356–366.

Wellisch, D. K., Vincent, J. P., & Ro-Trock, G. K. (1976). Family therapy versus individual therapy: A study of adolescents and their parents. In Olson, D. (Ed.), *Treating relationships* pp. 275–302. Lake Mills, IA: Graphic Press.

West, D. J. (1969). *Present conduct and future delinquency.* London: Heineman.

West, D. J., & Farrington, D.P. (1973). *Who becomes delinquent?* London: Heineman.

Wiltz, N., & Patterson, G. (1974). An evaluation of parent training procedures designed to alter inappropriate aggressive behavior of boys. *Behavior Therapy, 5,* 215–221.

Winter, W. D., & Ferreira, A. J. (1969). Talking time as an index of intrafamilial similarity in normal and abnormal families. *Journal of Abnormal Psychology, 74,* 574–575.

Wood, K. M. (1978). Casework effectiveness: A new look at the research evidence. *Social Work, 23,* 437–458.

Zimberoff, S. J. (1968). Behavior modification with delinquents. *Correctional Psychologist, 3,* 11–25.

Zucker, H. J. (1943). Affectional identification and delinquency. *Archives of Psychology, 286,* 1–60.

INDEX

Adolescent, 157–168, 195, 199
Adolescent peer group, 54
Aichhorn, A., 13
Ainsworth, M., 13
Akers, R., 25, 26
Alexander, J., 58, 60, 63, 92–96, 97, 137
Alfaro, J., 23, 29
Alvord, J., 81, 91
Andrew, J., 15, 18
Andry, R., 20, 21, 27
Archer, Billy (case vignette), 183–186
Assessment, 146, 155, 157, 208, 211, 212, 213, 217
Ayres, B., 42

Bahr, S., 10, 14, 33
Bambrick, A., 104–105, 141
Bandura, A., 21

Baron, R., 116, 138
Barrs, C., 136, 140
Barton, C., 60
Beal, D., 118, 139
Becker, H., 14
"Behavior contracting", 89–92, 156, 175
"Behavior management training", 85–89
Behavioral theory, 51, 54, 56, 84–97, 137, 145–146, 150, 152–153
Berk, R., 17, 18
Berleman, W., 52
Biles, D., 15
Birchler, G., 145
Birth order, 14, 15
Blumenfeld, H., 132, 144
Boston, M., 13
Bowlby, J., 13, 20
Brim, O., 47